Establishing
in
Las Vegas

Revised Edition

"The Inside Scoop"
Everything you need to know!
by
Ruth Catalano

Copyright 1992
Ruth Catalano

Revised Edition
Copyright 1994

Published by:
Information and Assistance Network
3675 Rainbow Blvd.
Suite 107, Box 122
Las Vegas, NV 89103

This book is dedicated to
all the people who 'think' they might
want to live in Las Vegas,
and to all my supportive friends
who said, "Wow! I wish I had
had this book when I moved here."

Special thanks for the research help
given me by long-time Las Vegans -
Ellen Thomas, Michael Phelan,
Bob Phelan, Billie West, Donna Hall,
Roy Fehler, Bob Ippilito,
Judy Riley, and Al and Leona Milbrath.

And an extra special
"Thank You" to my husband, John,
who insisted we move to
Las Vegas in 1970.
Without him, this book would
not have come into existence.

The first edition of *Getting Established in Las Vegas* was published in 1992. Since that time, there have been so many changes in the city that this "Revised Edition" became necessary. During the past two years, I have spoken with literally hundreds of people who have recently moved to Las Vegas. They have asked for additional information in many areas which I had not covered in the previous book.

With this revised edition, I will try to cover all the bases. However, changes do occur, daily, so please bear with us if some bit of information is not quite accurate at the time you read this.

CONTENTS

Introduction 1
Welcome to Las Vegas 13
Taxes in Nevada 14
Traveling to My Future 16
Airports and Airlines 16
Las Vegas Hotels 20
Hotels and Casinos 21
Hotels - Non-Gaming 29
Opening a Bank Account 33
Apartments for Rent 38
Homes in Las Vegas 63
New Homes - Areas and Price Range 67
Getting a Mortgage 76
Mobile Home Parks 81
Utilities 82
Department of Motor Vehicles 94
Your Personal Cost Worksheet 100
Employment 105
Areas of Job Expertise Needed 117

The Employment Agency	119
Casino Jobs	121
Average Salaries	125
Trade Schools	127
The Las Vegas Convention and Visitors Authority	133
Opening a Business in Clark County	137
Business Licensing	140
Las Vegas Chamber of Commerce & Nevada Development Authority	145
Business Advertising Budget	147
Clark County School District	151
University of Nevada, Las Vegas	156
Community College of Southern Nevada	158
Seniors	160
Senior Health Care	163
Stretching Your Social Security	164
Getting Married in Las Vegas	170
Valet This & Valet That	173
Shopping	176
Grocery Shopping	179

Beating the Recession	180
Public Transportation	184
Hospitals	187
Rehabilitation Hospitals	189
Favorites	191
Breakfast Specials	195
Buffets	198
Dining Guide to Las Vegas Restaurants	208
Churches	259
Las Vegas and Its "Suburbs"	263
Nellis Air Force Base	266
Recreation	270
Sporting Areas	278
Golf Courses	279
Social and Charitable Organizations	286
Automobile Renting and Leasing	289
Driving With Caution	289
Miscellaneous Information	291
A Las Vegas Success Story	292
How It All Started	295

INTRODUCTION

Having lived and worked in Las Vegas for over 23 years, I have had the privilege of meeting people from all over the world. During the past eight years, I have owned a business which has brought many newcomers through my doors. In meeting with them, my employees and I have dispensed with countless hours of information and assistance. As in any new city to which you may move, there is always some confusion and frustration. Where can I go to acquire certain things or who can I call to get things done? There are also reports of bad experiences and unexpected costs.

I suddenly realized that there was a very real need for a total directory on everything a newcomer to Las Vegas should know, including all the costs involved, and details on the housing, job, and business markets.

I am not a literary giant. My writing tends to be more like a letter to a friend. Occasionally, I get carried away with flowery phrases that drive editors crazy, but I'm not writing for them. I'm writing for friends who want to know about the "real" Las Vegas. At times, I sound as though I am prejudiced, but that's because I am. Las Vegas has been very good to my family. We had a rough start in 1970. There were ups and downs throughout the years. We struggled, learned a lot, and survived. We have owned successful businesses, had good jobs and nice homes, and made many wonderful friends. We are very proud of Las Vegas and of the great progress this city has made. It's a wonderful place to visit and an even greater place to live. It is "home!" Perhaps when you finish reading this book, you will consider making it your home too.

WELCOME TO LAS VEGAS!!!

♥ ♣ ♦ ♠ ♥ ♣ ♦ ♠

QUESTION

Why do people move to Las Vegas at the rate of thousands per month?

ANSWER

1. Climate - Temperatures are normally mild (60's - 80's) approximately nine months out of the year. During the summer months, the temperatures sometimes climb as high as 110 - 115 degrees. However, on those days the local people either relax in their pools, or stay in their air-conditioned homes or offices. They also drive cars which are air-conditioned. The average temperature for the winter of 1993-94 was 45 degrees, and by February 27, 1994, we were at 70 degrees.

2. Shoveling snow is unheard of.

3. No state income tax.

4. Low property taxes.

5. There is an abundance of "Dining Out" bargains all around town. Many hotels offer full breakfasts for 99¢, and fabulous buffet lunches and dinners that range from $3.00 and up. It almost makes dining out cheaper than cooking at home. (That's what I tell my husband all the time.)

6. There is a vast amount of entertainment offered throughout the city, including sporting events.

7. There are numerous golf courses, bowling centers, and tennis courts throughout the area, in addition to boating and fishing at Lake Mead, and snow skiing at Mt. Charleston.

8. The University of Nevada, Las Vegas is listed as one of the up and coming universities in the United States, giving a high quality education at a very reasonable price.

9. Home prices are very reasonable as compared to California, the East, and many parts of the Midwest and South.

10. Utility rates are relatively low, as compared to most metropolitan areas of the United States.

11. Good business climate - No state income tax.

12. Low unemployment figures - There are usually jobs for those who really want to work. Las Vegas had the lowest unemployment rate in the country as of December 1993.

13. And then there are those people who move to Las Vegas just to gamble. A vast majority of these people don't seem to remain as permanent residents. They have, however, contributed to establishing beautiful schools for Nevada. You see, our state gaming taxes help support our local school system, in addition to many other things.

Do any of these answers interest you? If so, start packing your bags and come on out. Las Vegas is the hospitality city and you will find more than enough to do and see.

This is a step-by-step guide on costs and what you should know if you are making a move to Las Vegas. Following these steps can save you countless hours of time, energy, money and aggravation.

♥ ♣ ♦ ♠ ♥ ♣ ♦ ♠

MELTING POT U.S.A.

There have been many stories of unusual, heartwarming meetings in Las Vegas, long lost friends and neighbors finding each other unexpectedly.

One such story that we witnessed happened back in 1979 when the Las Vegas-Chicagoans Club held one of their monthly social meetings. There were approximately 300 ex-Chicagoans in attendance. During the course of the meeting, the President asked each non-member to stand and introduce himself. She asked that they also tell the audience from what area of Chicagoland they hailed. When a guest in the front of the room introduced herself, a member who was seated in the far back jumped up and excitedly called out the guest's name. Those two ladies had been next door neighbors twenty years ago and hadn't seen each other since then. There were a lot of happy tears shed that evening.

* * * * * * *

At another of the Chicago Club meetings, when a "Happy Wedding Anniversary" was wished to a couple who had recently joined, another member moved in to get a better look. The name sounded terribly familiar to her. When she introduced herself to the couple, they all realized that she had been a bridesmaid in their large wedding party in Chicago forty years before.

* * * * * * *

Recently, a very beautiful Las Vegas model was at a retail store in Las Vegas taking part in a commercial which was being filmed. During the filming break, she began wandering through the store. She noticed a customer who she thought she knew. She approached the lady and introduced herself. She said, "I seem to know you from somewhere." The two had carried on a very short conversation when it dawned on them that they knew each other through a department store in Houston, Texas. Both of them had worked there at the same time ten years ago. It seems the model bought all of her cosmetics from the head cosmetologist at the store, who just happened to be this lady who was standing before her now. Each of them had moved to Las Vegas within the past five years.

* * * * * * *

In another incident, a gentleman was shopping in a Las Vegas furniture store when he heard a familiar voice. He looked to see who was speaking and found it was his old friend and neighbor from 27 years ago. The "voice" was that of the furniture store owner. After a hardy handshake and a little conversation, the man, who had just recently moved to Las Vegas, learned that the store owner had moved to Las Vegas twenty years ago. The man gave his new address to the owner and it turned out that these two gentlemen were neighbors again. The man's home, which he had just purchased, was only two blocks from his old friend.

* * * * * * *

In still another incident, a lady attended a banquet at one of the major hotels. She began staring at the banquet manager, and told her husband, "I know that man." Her husband looked and agreed, "Yes, he does look familiar." After the party, she approached the gentleman and said, "You look very familiar to my husband and me, but we can't place how we know you." After a long discussion, they came to the conclusion that they hadn't met before. The banquet manager was new to Las Vegas. The cities he had worked in previously were not on the couple's travel routes. He said, "And prior to that, I was born and raised in Bombay, India." The lady then related to him that she and her husband had traveled there 22 years before. At that time, this gentleman would have been eight years old. She proceeded to tell the banquet manager about the very nice gentleman they were able to secure to guide them all around Bombay. The young man smiled and said, "It's a possibility that your guide could have been my father because that's what he did for a living back then." The lady was amazed! She asked the young man if he resembled his father. He replied, "Yes, I look just like him!" She remembered that in her travel photo albums she had a picture of her husband with the tour guide from Bombay. She promised the banquet manager that she would return one day soon, with the picture, so they could see if it was his father. She did, and it was! The young man explained that his father had passed away three years earlier, and it was really nice to meet someone in the United States who knew him and spoke so highly of him. The couple and the young man have become exceedingly good friends and plan to travel to India together where the young man will then serve as their tour guide.

****

Then there are those unexpected moments of recognizing someone you know you've seen before. On rare occasions, some of these recognitions have resulted in "Unsolved Mysteries" and "America's Most Wanted", catching the suspect right here in Las Vegas. Although that has not been a common occurrence, it has happened a few times. Maybe it's because Las Vegas really is a "melting pot", but then again, maybe it's because Las Vegans are a more alert group of people.

RESIDENTS SAY...

"My husband and I left Minot, North Dakota, 6½ years ago, very eager to leave our snow shovels behind. We were both lucky to find jobs right away. I think what made our decision to move here was the weather and the nice people."

- Julie Jensen

"I left Detroit four years ago because I couldn't stand the weather anymore. I was a single mother. I wanted to start a new life. I have opened my own restaurant. What I love most about Las Vegas is seeing the sun shine."

- Lorraine Rustom

"I was born and raised in Chicago and couldn't get out of it fast enough. One more winter and I would have died! There is no town like Las Vegas. I love the people, the weather, and I can grocery shop at midnight if I want. After 18 years, I still love it!"

- D. Maiola

"After being caught in a Los Angeles traffic jam for <u>six</u> hours trying to get from Los Angeles International Airport to Dana Point (approximately 50 miles), I was thrilled to move to a city where you can get from one side of the city to the other, in less than thirty minutes!"

- Linda Corby

"My wife and I left Colorado Springs, Colorado, six years ago. The main reason was because of the jobs. I haven't had problems finding work as a plumber. This town has been very good to us. We love the town being open 24 hours and all the great places to eat."

- Harold Call

"My husband and I left California two years ago. The pace and the taxes were too much. We love everything about Las Vegas - the people, great restaurants, and the weather."

- Ricki Canham

"I feel that I'm alive today because of Las Vegas. I left Minnesota due to health problems seven years ago. My doctor recommended a warm, dry climate. I've never felt better and I am enjoying every day of my life at age 74. Not only am I physically better, but I'm emotionally healthy because I have so much to keep me busy and active here."

- P. Rasmussen

♥ ♣ ♦ ♠ ♥ ♣ ♦ ♠

WELCOME TO LAS VEGAS!

Nevada is bordered by California on the west and south, Utah and Arizona on the east, and Idaho and Oregon to the north. Las Vegas sits in the southeast corner of the state, approximately 300 miles from Los Angeles, and about 300 miles from Phoenix, Arizona.

The state's major growth industries throughout the years have been gaming, the military, and mining. (Yes, there is still gold in "them thar" hills!...or is it silver?!)

We had over 22 million visitors who traveled through McCarran Airport in 1993.

According to the United States Census Bureau (1994), Nevada has become the fastest growing state in the nation with Las Vegas being the fastest growing city. A vast majority of the new residents pouring into Las Vegas are retirees who are ready to enjoy life. Las Vegas offers them an abundance of ways to do that.

In 1991, our innovative Las Vegas residents elected their first woman mayor, Jan Laverty Jones. A graduate of Stanford University, she is an astute businesswoman who was involved in her family's auto dealerships prior to becoming mayor. During her first year in office, she gained popularity as she struggled to find solutions to many of the city's troubles. The people who deal with her on a daily basis are encouraged by her endless energy, her sense of humor, and her "down to earth" approach. She is also very active in the charitable community, and is dedicated to making Las Vegas a most desirable place to live. She has made great strides in trying to eliminate the "homeless" problem in Las Vegas too.

♥ ♣ ♦ ♠ ♥ ♣ ♦ ♠

TAXES IN NEVADA

More and more major corporations and businesses are moving to Nevada because of our favorable tax structure. The tax situation is also favorable to the individual as well, which has contributed to our vast population increase over the past several years. Our present sales tax is 7%. However, there is no tax on food items purchased for home.

For the individual, we have no state income tax, no personal property tax, and no inheritance gift tax. The property tax rate varies according to the area in which the home or property is purchased. An average rate would probably fall in the area of approximately $2.15 - $2.50 per $100 of assessed value. Many people moving here from other parts of the country report that not only are our homes lower priced, but the property taxes are too. The overall consensus of new residents is that most things in Las Vegas cost less than where they originally came from. That includes property, taxes, food, and clothing.

Businesses enjoy the following tax benefits: no corporate income tax, no franchise tax, no unitary tax, no inventory tax, no capital stock tax, and no admissions tax. We do have a "business tax" which amounts to roughly $25 per employee per quarter. Gaming tax revenues account for 40% of Nevada's budget, and taxes from tourism add another good percentage, thus allowing our state to hold down the amount of taxes that must be paid by the individual or businesses.

♥ ♣ ♦ ♠ ♥ ♣ ♦ ♠

TRAVELING TO MY NEW FUTURE

We are prejudice when it comes to naming the finest city in America. Therefore, it is up to you to travel to Las Vegas to formulate your own opinion. Never let it be said that we influenced you unduly.

An "inspection trip" should be your first step if you are thinking about possibly relocating to a new city. A minimum of three days should be planned for the trip to give you time to drive around, look around, and talk to people. If you can spare more time and stay longer, do so. It can only be to your advantage. The first step to your inspection trip is to contact an airline for rates and available flights.

AIRPORTS AND AIRLINES

McCarran International Airport is situated in the southeast section of Las Vegas. At one time, it was on the edge of the city, but with the rapid growth experienced, homes, offices and shopping centers have gone up all around it. It is located at 5795 South Paradise Road, and has been in a state of major expansion for several years. The result is a very attractive and efficient terminal. The place is also filled with many lovely shops. You can load up on souvenirs, or buy designer clothes if that's what you want. There are so many unique shops that you may want to spend an hour or two just browsing. If shopping is not your thing, there are always the slot machines to play!

The following is a list of the various airlines servicing Las Vegas:

* Adventure Airlines
  Aer Lingus
  Aerolineas Argentinas
  Air Canada
  Air Express
* Air Nevada
* Air Vegas, Inc.
  Alaska Airlines
  America West Airlines
  American Airlines
  American Trans Air
  Ana-All Nippon Airways
  British Airways
  Canadian Airlines
* Canyon Flyers
  China Airlines
  Continental
  Delta

Finnair
Grand Airways
Hawaiian Airlines
Japan Air Lines
KLM Royal Dutch Airlines
Korean Air
* Las Vegas Airlines
Mexicana
Midwest Express
Morris Airlines
Northwest
Pacific State Airlines
Quantas Airways
Scenic Airlines
Singapore Airlines
Skywest
Southwest
TWA
Trans Shuttle
Tri-Star
US Air
United Airlines
World Airways

Those airlines denoted with a * are mainly sightseeing aircraft which service areas such as the Grand Canyon and Lake Powell. Some of the airlines listed do not fly to Las

Vegas on a daily basis, but often have charters coming in from different cities.

Now that you have the list of the airlines which fly into Las Vegas, it is time to get on the phone and call the ones which also service your area. If you have a travel agent, it would be wise to call them. They can assist in making your airline reservation, your hotel reservation, and arrange for a rental car. With the sophisticated computers used, they can tell you which airlines and hotels have the best rates. They are also aware of tour companies which are offering terrific air/hotel packages, which can save a lot of money.

♥ ♣ ♦ ♠ ♥ ♣ ♦ ♠

LAS VEGAS HOTELS

Las Vegas is tourism and vacation-oriented. The usual trend is that the weekends find many hotel rooms full, as compared to a lower rate of occupancy during the week. The room rates at most hotels and motels are also usually higher on Friday and Saturday nights. The best idea for getting a good room rate is to plan your trip from Sunday through Thursday. There are nice rooms which can be had for $35 a night and up during that period. Many also offer special packages with even greater savings and a few free meals during Sunday through Thursday. Call the hotel to see if they have any special packages to offer for the date you are interested in.

The following is a listing of some of the hotels and motels which are listed in the Las Vegas Chamber of Commerce directory. There are many others that are equally as nice, which can be found in the telephone book yellow pages.

HOTELS AND CASINOS

ALGIERS HOTEL
2845 Las Vegas Blvd. South
Las Vegas, NV   89109
735-3311/No 800 #

ARIZONA CHARLIE'S HOTEL/CASINO
740 S. Decatur Boulevard
Las Vegas, NV   89107
258-5111/800-342-2695

BALLY'S CASINO RESORT
3645 Las Vegas Blvd. South
Las Vegas, NV   89109
739-4111/800-634-3434

BARBARY COAST HOTEL/CASINO
3595 Las Vegas Blvd. South
Las Vegas, NV   89109
737-7111/800-634-6755

BEST WESTERN MARDI GRAS INN
3500 Paradise Road
Las Vegas, NV   89109
731-2020/800-634-6501

BOARDWALK HOTEL CASINO
3750 Las Vegas Blvd. South
Las Vegas, NV   89109
735-1167/800-635-4581

CAESAR'S PALACE HOTEL/CASINO
3570 Las Vegas Blvd. South
Las Vegas, NV   89109
731-7110/800-634-6661

CALIFORNIA HOTEL
12 Ogden Avenue
Las Vegas, NV   89101
385-1222/800-634-6255

CIRCUS CIRCUS
2880 Las Vegas Blvd. South
Las Vegas, NV   89109
734-0410/800-634-3450

EL CORTEZ HOTEL/CASINO
600 Fremont
Las Vegas, NV   89101
385-5200/800-634-6703

EXCALIBUR HOTEL/CASINO
3850 Las Vegas Blvd. South
Las Vegas, NV   89119
597-7777/800-937-7777

FITZGERALD'S HOTEL/CASINO
    301 E. Fremont
    Las Vegas, NV   89101
    388-2400/800-274-LUCK

FLAMINGO HILTON HOTEL/CASINO
    3555 Las Vegas Blvd. South
    Las Vegas, NV   89109
    733-3111/800-732-2111

FOUR QUEENS HOTEL/CASINO
    202 E. Fremont
    Las Vegas, NV   89101
    385-4011/800-634-6045

FREMONT HOTEL/CASINO
    200 E. Fremont
    Las Vegas, NV   89101
    385-3232/800-634-6160

FRONTIER HOTEL/CASINO
    3120 Las Vegas Blvd. South
    Las Vegas, NV   89109
    794-8200/800-634-6966

GOLD COAST HOTEL/CASINO
    4000 W. Flamingo Road
    Las Vegas, NV   89103
    367-7111/800-331-5334

GOLDEN GATE HOTEL/CASINO
111 South Main
Las Vegas, NV   89101
382-3510/800-426-0521

HACIENDA RESORT HOTEL/CASINO
3950 Las Vegas Blvd. South
Las Vegas, NV   89119
739-8911/800-634-6713

HARRAH'S HOTEL/CASINO
3475 Las Vegas Blvd. South
Las Vegas, NV   89109
369-5000/800-634-6765

HOLIDAY ROYALE
4505 Paradise Road
Las Vegas, NV   89109
733-7676/800-732-7676

HOWARD JOHNSON LODGE/CASINO
3111 W. Tropicana
Las Vegas, NV   89103
798-1111/800-654-2000

IMPERIAL PALACE HOTEL/CASINO
3535 Las Vegas Blvd. South
Las Vegas, NV   89109
731-3311/800-634-6441

LADY LUCK HOTEL/CASINO
206 N. Third
Las Vegas, NV   89101
477-3000/800-523-9582

LAS VEGAS CLUB HOTEL/CASINO
18 E. Fremont
Las Vegas, NV   89101
385-1664/800-634-6532

LAS VEGAS HILTON HOTEL/CASINO
3000 Paradise Road
Las Vegas, NV   89109
732-5111/800-732-7117

LUXOR HOTEL/CASINO
3900 Las Vegas Blvd. South
Las Vegas, NV   89119
262-4000

MGM GRAND HOTEL/CASINO
3799 Las Vegas Blvd. South
Las Vegas, NV   89109
891-7777/800-929-1111

MIRAGE HOTEL/CASINO
3400 Las Vegas Blvd. South
Las Vegas, NV   89109
791-7111/800-627-6667

PALACE STATION HOTEL/CASINO
2411 W. Sahara
Las Vegas, NV   89102
367-2411/800-634-3101

RIO SUITE HOTEL/CASINO
3700 W. Flamingo
Las Vegas, NV   89103
252-7777/800-888-1808

RIVIERA HOTEL/CASINO
2901 Las Vegas Blvd. South
Las Vegas, NV   89109
734-5110/800-634-6753

SAHARA HOTEL
2535 Las Vegas Blvd. South
Las Vegas, NV   89109
737-2111/800-634-6666

SAM'S TOWN HOTEL/CASINO
5111 Boulder Highway
Las Vegas, NV   89122
456-7777/800-634-6371

SANDS HOTEL/CASINO
3355 Las Vegas Blvd. South
Las Vegas, NV   89109
733-5000/800-634-6901

**SHERATON DESERT INN
HOTEL/CASINO**
3145 Las Vegas Blvd. South
Las Vegas, NV   89109
733-4444/800-634-6906

SHOWBOAT HOTEL/CASINO
2800 Fremont
Las Vegas, NV   89104
385-9123/800-826-2800

STARDUST HOTEL/CASINO
3000 Las Vegas Blvd. South
Las Vegas, NV   89109
732-6111/800-824-6757

THUNDERBIRD HOTEL/CASINO
1213 Las Vegas Blvd. South
Las Vegas, NV   89104
384-4444/800-322-0075

TREASURE ISLAND HOTEL/CASINO
3300 Las Vegas Blvd. South
Las Vegas, NV   89109
894-7111

TROPICANA RESORT/CASINO
3801 Las Vegas Blvd. South
Las Vegas, NV   89119
739-2222/800-634-4000

UNION PLAZA HOTEL/CASINO
1 South Main
Las Vegas, NV   89101
386-2110/800-634-6575

VACATION VILLAGE HOTEL/CASINO
6711 Las Vegas Blvd. South
Las Vegas, NV   89119
897-1700/800-338-0608

VEGAS WORLD HOTEL/CASINO
2000 Las Vegas Blvd. South
Las Vegas, NV   89104
382-2000/800-634-6277

WESTERN HOTEL/CASINO
899 E. Fremont
Las Vegas, NV   89101
384-4620/800-634-6703

WESTWARD HO HOTEL/CASINO
2900 Las Vegas Blvd. South
Las Vegas, NV   89109
731-2900/800-634-6803

HOTELS - NON-GAMING

ALEXIS PARK HOTEL
375 E. Harmon
Las Vegas, NV   89109
796-3300/800-582-2228

THE FAIRFIELD INN BY MARIOTT
3850 Paradise Road
Las Vegas, NV   89109
791-0899/800-228-2800

HOWARD JOHNSON PLAZA SUITE
4255 Paradise Road
Las Vegas, NV   89109
369-4400/800-654-2000

RAMADA SUITE - ST. TROPEZ HOTEL
455 E. Harmon
Las Vegas, NV   89109
369-5400/800-666-5400

♥ ♣ ♦ ♠ ♥ ♣ ♦ ♠

The last three months of 1993 were "Grand Opening" time for three new exotic theme hotels: Treasure Island, with 2400 rooms and a pirate atmosphere; the Luxor, with 2536 rooms and Egyptian decor; and the MGM Grand, with 5000 rooms and a large theme park for the family. That brings Las Vegas to 86,053 hotel rooms available in the city. It also added 12,000 jobs to our employment records. Construction is on a fast pace here with many other hotels, apartments, and homes being built.

♥ ♣ ♦ ♠ ♥ ♣ ♦ ♠

A "MOVING TO LAS VEGAS" STORY
(The names have been changed
to protect the guilty)

When Bobby, from Rhode Island, told his wife, Doris, that he wanted to move to Las Vegas, her first reaction was, "You're not sticking me in this barren desert". That was in 1959, while on a visit to his brother who was living in Las Vegas. Unknown to Bobby's wife, he had already quit his job in Rhode Island before they left on vacation. He had every intention of moving west. Seeing Doris' negative reaction to the small, dusty town, he agreed to go on to California to visit another brother. He would see if he could acquire a job there.

Although they liked the greenery of California, the job prospects were very limited. After a few months, they had run out of money. All they had was a full tank of gas and a promise of a job in Las Vegas. They headed back. The problem was, the "full" tank of gas was not quite "full" enough. They ran out in Baker, California. They had no money, so Bobby offered to leave Doris, their small daughter, and his spare tire with the gas station owner, if the man would give him gas to get to Vegas. He promised the man he would get money from his brother and return to pay. The gas station owner "gave" him the gas without holding Doris, the daughter, OR the spare tire, hostage. He said, "The next time you come through Baker, you can pay me."

They never forgot this kindness. Upon their arrival in Las Vegas, a job as a chef materialized. When Bobby's first paycheck arrived, he gave the gas money to his brother, who was driving to Los Angeles. He asked him to stop in Baker. When the brother stopped to pay the gas station owner, the man refused the money. You see, the brother was part of the Louis Prima band. Louis, his wife, and the whole group got out to thank the gas station owner. He was thrilled. After acquiring their autograph, he said "that" was payment enough. As years rolled by, Bobby and Doris kept in touch with the man, and whenever he came to Las Vegas, he always stopped to visit them.

Although their first years in Las Vegas were very lean financially, Bobby and Doris worked hard and struggled to get ahead. Eventually, Bobby entered the gaming industry and slowly forged to the top. Twenty-five years later, he retired from his position as an Executive Vice President for a major hotel. That was before he was 50 years old. Yes, dreams do come true in Las Vegas...if you work hard enough.

♥ ♣ ♦ ♠ ♥ ♣ ♦ ♠

OPENING A BANK ACCOUNT

So you've arrived in town with your cashiers check from your hometown bank. You're ready to open a bank account and spend your money...only there could be a little problem with that. Cashiers checks could be lost or stolen, therefore most local banks place a five to ten day hold on the check before it is officially cleared by your previous bank. Some banks will offer you the courtesy of calling your bank (you pay for the call) to clear it with a bank officer there. If the official clearance is given, you are then allowed to write checks from your new account immediately. Sometimes it is worth the price of the phone call, especially if you have to begin giving deposits for your utilities and your new residence.

For many years, Las Vegas was a very transient town. People moved here thinking they were going to walk into a casino job with no experience. When they were hit with the fact that they needed training first, they often were left short of funds. Their next step was to get some extra money by gambling. (That's how all of our hotels and casinos have been able to expand and remodel!) Needless to say, their funds usually ended up becoming even "shorter", so many wrote rubber checks which bounced sky high. Then they would leave town. Due to this unique, but ever-occurring, incident, the Nevada banks were forced to take some drastic measures. One of these was the Check Guarantee Card. That lovely little piece of plastic has become almost a "must-have" in Las Vegas. What it does is guarantee to the person or business who is accepting your check that the bank will fully guarantee payment of your check, whether you have the funds in the account or not. The usual amount of the guarantee by the bank is for approximately $500 in merchandise.

You should apply for your check guarantee card when you open your bank account. You will need to complete a credit application for it. The bank will then check your previous credit history to determine if you are credit-worthy. Allow three to four weeks, normally, for your guarantee card to be sent to you. If you have a history of writing bad checks, the chances are you won't be given a bank guarantee card. If your credit shows that you haven't written bad checks, but you have been slow in paying bills, the Las Vegas bank may delay giving you a guarantee card for six months to a year. This will give them a chance to see how you handle your account with them. If you can't get a guarantee card right away, you may be forced to carry cash when you go to the grocery store or wherever you may wish to shop. Most merchants absolutely insist on seeing the guarantee card, along with your Nevada driver's license, when taking a check from you. The only other option, besides paying by cash, is to use a credit card, if you have one, and if the merchant will accept it.

When opening a bank account in Las Vegas, two forms of identification must be presented for each person who will be a signer on the account. That is the requirement for a personal account, as well as a business or corporate account. Opening a corporate account will require your Federal I.D. number, along with your Articles of Incorporation. To open a business partnership account, you will need your Federal I.D. number, along with a copy of your partnership papers. If you are opening a business account and you are the sole proprietor, you will have to present the papers which you filed with the Clark County Clerk's Office for a "Fictitious Firm Name". Some banks will allow you to fill out the papers for a fictitious name at their bank and they will file it for you with the Clerk's Office. That paperwork takes about two weeks to clear. It saves you a trip, making it one less place you have to stop when opening a business. Not all of the banks will do that, however, so you should check with your bank. You may be able to get that information just by calling them.

How many checks you order from the bank, when you open your account, will determine the charges which will be on your opening bank statement. Don't forget to deduct that charge from your checkbook the first month. Some banks charge a monthly service charge in conjunction with the amount of money that is in your account. Ask about the service charges when opening your account. They vary from bank to bank. Several of the local banks offer special packages to senior citizens (i.e., no check charges, no service charges, etc.), so if you are a senior, inquire about that also.

Since Las Vegas has a bank on practically every corner, it is very easy to do your banking. Most are closed on weekends and holidays, but practically all of them have ATM machines, open 24 hours. You can make deposits, make loan payments, or get cash from the ATM machines. A few of the banks are open on Saturday mornings, and some stay open until 6:00 PM. Again, since this varies from bank to bank, you must check with the bank you are interested in.

Since a gentleman from Saudi Arabia scolded me for not including the names of the major banks in the first edition of *Getting Established in Las Vegas*, I will include them now, for those who have lots of money to deposit. The following banks will welcome you (most of them will welcome you too, even if you start out with just a little bit of money!):

>American Bank of Commerce
>American Federal Savings
>Bank of America
>Citibank of Nevada
>California Federal Bank
>Comstock Bank
>First Interstate Bank
>First Security Bank
>Nevada State Bank
>Pioneer Citizens Bank
>Pri-Merit Bank
>Security Pacific
>Sun State Bank
>U.S. Bank

♥ ♣ ♦ ♠ ♥ ♣ ♦ ♠

APARTMENTS FOR RENT

Many people relocating to Las Vegas begin by moving into an apartment. If that is your intention, the following list should be helpful to you. We have listed the apartment complexes by areas of the city.

Since new apartment complexes are constantly being built, it is difficult to keep this list current. Go to a local convenience store when in Las Vegas and pick up a copy of the For Rent Magazine. It is free and will be most helpful. Their toll-free number is 1-800-420-0040, or write to: For Rent Magazine, 7330 Smoke Ranch Road, Suite A, Las Vegas, NV 89128.

SOUTHWEST LAS VEGAS AREA

APARTMENT ADDRESS	TELEPHONE (702)	BEDROOMS BATHROOMS	PRICE RANGE
Alpine Village 901 Brush	870-3044	1-2-3 1-2	$450- $695
Banbury Cross 3150 S. Decatur	876-2923	1-2-3 1-1½	$420- $635
Barcelona Apartments 3011 S. Arville	876-0929	2-3 1-2	$435- $545
Cameron Apartments 4600 W. Sirius	871-3009	1-2 1	$430- $490
Casablanca Apartments 5110 S. Jones	252-7044	1-2 1-2	$560- $670
Cypress Point 5275 W. Tropicana	873-4181	1-2 1-2	$545- $645
Flamingo Road 5795 W. Flamingo	368-2644	2 2	$669
Grand View 4255 W. Viking	362-1910	1-2-3 1-2	$385- $645

SOUTHWEST LAS VEGAS (CONT')

APARTMENT ADDRESS	TELEPHONE (702)	BEDROOMS BATHROOMS	PRICE RANGE
Hidden Cove 3335 Hauk	876-3433	1-2 1-2	$435- $725
Indian Hills 4550 W. Sahara	878-4820	1-2 1-2	$560- $680
Meadows Court 2692 Redrock	252-8700	1-2 1-2	$495- $610
Pebble Cove 5101 O'Bannon	876-1211	1-2-3 1-2	$500- $725
Pennview Apartments 3820 Pennwood	876-0550	2-3 1-2	$400- $498
Renaissance Villas 5419 W. Tropicana	367-1001	1-2 1-2	$545- $635
The Ritz 4250 S. Jones	362-7599	1-2 1-2	$525- $595
Sahara Palms 2900 El Camino Avenue	873-6887	1-2-2 2	$460- $680

SOUTHWEST LAS VEGAS (CONT')

APARTMENT ADDRESS	TELEPHONE (702)	BEDROOMS BATHROOMS	PRICE RANGE
Shadow Brook 3851 S. Wynn Road	871-1683	1-2 1-2	$470-$525
Shadow Ridge 3200 S. Arville	362-6190	1-2 2	$465-$710
Shelter Cove 2683 S. Decatur	362-4852	1-2 1-2	$485-$680
Silverado Village 3750 S. Arville	362-9373	1-2-3 1-2	$455-$710
Spanish Oaks 2301 S. Valley View	873-1833	1-2 1	$475-$525
The Springs 3663 S. Valley View	871-8886	1-2 1-2	$415-$570
St. Tropez Villa 4151 W. Sirius	873-0565	1-2 1-2	$430-$520
Sundance Village 6500 W. Charleston	870-1982	1-2-3 1-2	$435-$670

SOUTHWEST LAS VEGAS (CONT')

APARTMENT ADDRESS	TELEPHONE (702)	BEDROOMS BATHROOMS	PRICE RANGE
Sunpointe 2870 S. Decatur	362-0642	1-2 1½-2	$410- $495
Twain Estates 3651 Arville	367-6330	S-1-2 1-2½	$435- $600
Whispering Waters 4155 W. Twain	367-8789	1-2 1-2	$455- $515
Winsome West 5050 S. Duneville	364-1236	1-2 1-2	$450- $525
Woodcreek Apartments 4485 Pennwood	873-2598	1-2-3 1-2	$425- $650
Woodhaven Apartments 3650 Stober	876-8902	1-2 1	$410- $475
WoodLake Villas 4747 Pennwood	367-3669	1-2 1-2	$475- $590
Wyandotte Apartments 2629 Wyandotte	876-2122	1-2 1	$415 $500

THE LAKES AREA
(West of Rainbow and Sahara)

APARTMENT ADDRESS	TELEPHONE (702)	BEDROOMS BATHROOMS	PRICE RANGE
Anchor Village 8600 Starboard	363-8033	1-2-3 1-2	$500- $710
The Breakers 9901 W. Sahara	254-3133	1-2 1-2	$550- $675
Club Pacific 9325 W. Desert Inn	254-2582	2-3 2	$690- $795
The Enclaves 8455 W. Sahara	363-9700	1-3 1-2	$590- $930
Sky Court Harbors Desert Inn W. of Durango	255-0782	1-3 1-2	$565- $800
Summerhill Pointe 9501 W. Sahara	254-7777	1-2-3 1-2	$545- $765

♥ ♣ ♦ ♠ ♥ ♣ ♦ ♠

SOUTHEAST LAS VEGAS AREA

APARTMENT ADDRESS	TELEPHONE (702)	BEDROOMS BATHROOMS	PRICE RANGE
Avanti Park 1161 Lulu	736-6263	1-2-3 1-2	$450- $650
Boulevard Park 1374 E. Desert Inn	735-1397	2-3 1-2	$475- $600
Brittney Heights 4855 Vegas Valley	454-4979	1-2-3 1-2	$495- $710
Camelot Apartments 5088 Maryland Pkwy	798-0004	1-2 1	$375- $425
Canyon Club 2665 S. Bruce	735-0624	1-2-3 1-2	$440- $540
Carriage Park Villas 2831 Wheelwright	641-6000	2 2	$550
Charlestonwood 2900 E. Charleston	386-0277	S-1-2 1	$350- $455
Clarkdale Arms 2417 Wengert	382-4510	1-2 1-2	$365- $400

SOUTHEAST LAS VEGAS (CONT')

APARTMENT ADDRESS	TELEPHONE (702)	BEDROOMS BATHROOMS	PRICE RANGE
Club Pacific at Flamingo 3145 E. Flamingo	454-2582	2-3 2	$695- $825
Coral Gardens 4475 Jimmy Durante	458-6827	S-1-2-3 1-2	$350- $610
Country Hills 5400 S. Maryland Parkway	798-1044	1-3 1-2	$475- $675
Crystal Court 900 E. Desert Inn	737-5597	1-2 1-2	$720- $965
Dana Pointe 1305 E. Rawhide	878-0919	1 1	$450
Desert Pointe 3255 E. Desert Inn	735-9566	1 1	$545
Desert Spa Gardens 5101 E. Twain	458-3866	1-2 1-2	$450- $555
Emerald Bay 4701 E. Sahara	457-5400	1-2 1-2	$485- $595

SOUTHEAST LAS VEGAS (CONT')

APARTMENT ADDRESS	TELEPHONE (702)	BEDROOMS BATHROOMS	PRICE RANGE
Escondido Manor 4280 Escondido	731-5860	S-1 1	$350- $400
Foxwood Village 5050 Tamarus	736-7921	1-2-3 1-2	$460- $725
Karen East 3121 E. Karen	457-9399	S-1 1	$390- $410
King Arthur's Court 2650 Sherwood	735-2376	S-1-2 1	$365- $450
La Villita 1550 E. Harmon	731-5194	1-2 1-2	$390- $450
Lake Sahara 2500 Karen Avenue	457-3020	S-1-2 1-2	$385- $535
Limetree 2433 Clifford	382-0120	1 1	$360
Maryland Manor 5035 S. Maryland Parkway	736-4304	1-2 1-2	$395- $450

SOUTHEAST LAS VEGAS (CONT')

APARTMENT ADDRESS	TELEPHONE (702)	BEDROOMS BATHROOMS	PRICE RANGE
Newport Cove East 5272 Tamarus	736-7620	2 2	$695
Pacific Harbors at Flamingo 4050 Pacific Harbors Dr.	731-0159	1-3 1-2	$620- $780
Pacific Harbors at Stonegate 2988 Juniper Hills	641-5060	1-3 1-2	$540- $720
Paradise Square 4801 Harrison	456-6525	S-1-2-3 1-2	$375- $690
The Park Apartments 1600 E. Rochelle	733-7795	1-2-3 1-2	$439- $700
Park East 508 San Pablo	735-3380	S-1 1	$320- $365
Park Forest 50 North 21st	384-0294	S-1 1	$320- $340
Pinewood Apartments 3600 Swenson	734-6862	S-1-2-3 1-2	$355- $660

SOUTHEAST LAS VEGAS (CONT')

APARTMENT ADDRESS	TELEPHONE (702)	BEDROOMS BATHROOMS	PRICE RANGE
Reno Villas 5055 Jeffreys	736-2302	1-2 1-2	$450- $570
Riverbend Village 3937 S. Spencer	737-0488	1-2-3 1-2	$475- $750
Roberts Rancheros 1324 Elizabeth	736-1090	1 1	$415
Roman Villas 3665 Cambridge	732-4859	1-2 1-2	$430- $500
Sahara Gardens 4801 E. Sahara	457-9055	1-2-3 1-2	$450- $630
Sandpiper Village 3955 S. Algonquin	731-1066	1-2-3 1-2	$450- $725
Saratoga Palms 3850 Mountain Vista	458-8041	1-2-3 1-2	$450- $660
Southgate Apartments 5550 S. Maryland Pkwy	798-6688	S-1-2 1-2	$430- $575

SOUTHEAST LAS VEGAS (CONT')

APARTMENT ADDRESS	TELEPHONE (702)	BEDROOMS BATHROOMS	PRICE RANGE
Stonegate Courts 5075 Spyglass Hill Drive	641-2501	1-2 1-2	$525- $625
Stonegate Greens 5150 Spyglass Hill Drive	641-3641	1-2 1-2	$529- $619
Sun Chase 3200 McLeod	369-1112	S-1-2 1-2	$465- $599
Sunrise Springs 4455 E. Twain	435-0050	1-2-3 1-2	$525- $730
Sunset Springs 6930 Paradise	361-0694	1-2-3 1-2	$495- $745
Tropicana Royale 1900 E. Tropicana	798-5519	1-2-3 1-2	$485- $685
Tropicana Village 4995 S. Maryland Pkwy	739-7916	1-2-3 1-2	$440- $675
Veracruz 5325 E. Tropicana	435-1993	1-2-3 1-2	$515- $759

SOUTHEAST LAS VEGAS (CONT')

APARTMENT ADDRESS	TELEPHONE (702)	BEDROOMS BATHROOMS	PRICE RANGE
Viking Villas 1500 E. Viking	794-4500	1-2 1-2	$389- $699
The Village at Karen 2709 Alicia Lynn	457-4959	2 1	$540
Villas de Mission East 5055 E. Charleston	459-2202	1-2-3 1-2	$475- $685
Villas de Mission 1455 E. Katie	733-2994	1-2-3 1-2	$485- $720
The Virginia Apartments 5350 E. Tropicana	451-6900	1-2-3 1-1½	$420- $630
Winchester Woods 3135 S. Mojave	732-2522	1-2 1-2	$520- $620
Windridge 3040 E. Charleston	457-4004	S-1 1	$370- $435

♥ ♣ ♦ ♠ ♥ ♣ ♦ ♠

LAS VEGAS STRIP AREA

APARTMENT ADDRESS	TELEPHONE (702)	BEDROOMS BATHROOMS	PRICE RANGE
Barclay Square 3535 Cambridge Street	732-1081	1-3 1-2	$455- $730
Cobblestone Creek 4200 S. Paradise	731-2004	1-2 1-2	$475- $610
Desert Club 3950 Koval	732-1244	S-1-2 1-2	$535- $700
Greystone Park 2635 Karen Court	735-3308	S-3 1-2	$340- $600
International Villas 4630 Koval	732-2584	1-2-3 1-2	$600- $775
Las Palmas 3550 Paradise	732-8900	S-1-2 1-2	$475- $695
Mark I Apartments 1020 E. Desert Inn	732-2407	S-1-2 1-2	$500- $800
The Oasis 5316-C Danville	739-9410	1-2 1-2	$530- $620

LAS VEGAS STRIP (CONT')

APARTMENT ADDRESS	TELEPHONE (702)	BEDROOMS BATHROOMS	PRICE RANGE
Paradise Bay Club 4185 S. Paradise	796-3500	1-2 1-2	$530- $690
Sunlake Meadows 324 W. Cincinnati	598-0938	S-1-2 1-2	$325- $480

♥ ♣ ♦ ♠ ♥ ♣ ♦ ♠

NORTHWEST LAS VEGAS AREA

APARTMENT ADDRESS	TELEPHONE (702)	BEDROOMS BATHROOMS	PRICE RANGE
Catalina Shores at South Shore 2120 Jetty Rock Drive	363-9009	S-1-2-3 1-2	$555- $750
Canyon View 7400 Pirates Cove	254-2646	1-2-3 1-2	$540- $760
Club Pacific at the Shores 2200 Club Pacific Way	255-2582	2-3 1-2	$665- $790
Desert Park 100 Martin Luther King	383-0662	S-2 1	$375- $620
Diamondhead Apartments 1799 N. Decatur	647-9401	1-2 1-2	$535- $700
The Evergreen 5400 W. Cheyenne	645-6664	1-2 1-2	$465- $540
Fiesta! 210 Mission Laguna	258-4047	1-2 1-2	$540- $640
Fountains at Smoke Ranch 2300 Rock Springs	256-8006	1-2-3 1-2	$509- $730

NORTHWEST LAS VEGAS (CONT')

APARTMENT ADDRESS	TELEPHONE (702)	BEDROOMS BATHROOMS	PRICE RANGE
Laguna Shores 1800 N. Decatur	646-5011	2 2	$580
Mountain View Park 3201 Joanne Way	645-3006	1-2 1	$410- $460
Northpointe 3333 Michael Way	645-4321	1-2 1-2	$495- $560
Northridge Terrace 6016 Bromley	878-7978	1-2 1-2	$445- $510
Racquet Club 98 Martin Luther King	385-1193	S-1-2-3 1-2	$300- $610
Rainbow Gardens 6917 Lunarlight	255-9139	2-3 1-2	$720- $830
Shadow Hills 2121 N. Jones	647-7798	S-1 1	$405- $460
Spring Rainbow 100 N. Wallace	878-3100	1-2-3 1-2	$440- $655

NORTHWEST LAS VEGAS (CONT')

APARTMENT ADDRESS	TELEPHONE (702)	BEDROOMS BATHROOMS	PRICE RANGE
Spring Woods 4600 Vegas	648-1157	1-2 1-2	$450- $495
St. Croix Apartments 6661 Silverstream	877-0837	1-2 1-2	$520- $615
Sunterra Apartments 1901 N. Jones	646-3000	1-2-3 1-2	$460- $685
Torrey Springs 2200 Torrey Pines	647-9227	1-2-3 1-2	$500- $695
Westchase 2500 N. Rainbow	645-2203	1-2 2	$535- $635
Wildflower 6666 West Washington	877-0111	S-1-2-3 1-2	$395- $675

NORTHEAST LAS VEGAS AREA

APARTMENT ADDRESS	TELEPHONE (702)	BEDROOMS BATHROOMS	PRICE RANGE
Adobe Springs 451 N. Nellis	453-7368	1-2-3 1-2	$495- $710
Adobe Villas 3550 E. Lake Mead	452-2055	1-2-3 2	$395- $610
Brookstone Apartments 1401 N. Lamb	453-1577	1-2-3 1-2	$485- $695
Cape Cod Village 4231 Terrestial	438-0233	2 1	$530
Cedar Village 2850 E. Cedar	382-1680	1-2-3 1-2	$380- $540
Charleston Park 4840 E. Charleston	459-4207	1-2-3 1-2	$395- $545
Cheyenne Condo Apts. 3301 Civic Center Drive	642-3187	1-2-3 1-2	$395- $575
Eagle Trace 5370 E. Craig	643-3833	1-2-3 1-2	$540- $740

NORTHEAST LAS VEGAS (CONT')

APARTMENT ADDRESS	TELEPHONE (702)	BEDROOMS BATHROOMS	PRICE RANGE
Hilltop Apartments 601 North 13th Street	384-9272	2-3 1-2	$395- $495
Nellis Gardens 4255 N. Nellis	644-7772	1-2-3 1-2	$460- $650
Nellis Oasis 4870 Nellisoasis	644-1880	1-2-3 1-2	$480- $705
Northland Gardens 2950 N. Clifford	643-1391	1-2 1	$355- $375
Palm Village 1001 N. Pecos	399-5100	1-2-3 1-2	$395- $595
Sandy Lake 3650 E. Lake Mead	438-7363	1-2-3 1-2	$400- $625
Saratoga Palms 522 N. Lamb	452-4043	1-2-3 1-2	$430- $605
Spring Creeks 2851 E. Bonanza	598-0642	1-2-3 1-2	$455- $700

NORTHEAST LAS VEGAS (CONT')

APARTMENT ADDRESS	TELEPHONE (702)	BEDROOMS BATHROOMS	PRICE RANGE
Spring Lakes 3601 E. Bonanza	438-4140	1-2 1-2	$480- ?
Stewart Plaza 2611 E. Stewart	382-4902	2-3 1	$445- $495
Woodridge Villas 1591 Chartered Circle	399-1481	1-2-3 1-2	$460- $670

♥ ♣ ♦ ♠ ♥ ♣ ♦ ♠

GREEN VALLEY/HENDERSON AREAS

APARTMENT ADDRESS	TELEPHONE (702)	BEDROOMS BATHROOMS	PRICE RANGE
Copper Hills 981 Whitney Ranch Road	451-6494	2-3 1-2	$520- $780
Courtyards 5400 Mountain Vista	456-2900	S-1-2-3 1-2	$495- $790
Eiger Ridge 551 Eiger Way	454-4559	1-2 1-2	$515- $615
Green Valley Country Club 1770 Green Valley Pkwy	361-2263	1-2-3 1-2	$580- $810
Mandalay Bay 6650 S. Sandhill	451-8380	1-2-3 1-2	$475- $755
Mesa Club Apartments 6151 Mountain Vista	456-8400	1-2 1-2	$495- $650
Montego Bay 1050 Whitney Ranch Road	456-9009	1-2-3 1-2	$590- $820
Player's Club 1895 N. Green Valley Pkwy	361-3612	1-2 1-2	$585- $700

GREEN VALLEY/HENDERSON (CONT')

APARTMENT ADDRESS	TELEPHONE (702)	BEDROOMS BATHROOMS	PRICE RANGE
Pueblo Verde 2362 Green Valley Pkwy	456-0029	S-3 1-2	$465- $780
Village of Santa De La Paz 4375 E. Sunset	458-2229	1-2 1-2	$515- $595

♥ ♣ ♦ ♠ ♥ ♣ ♦ ♠

There are many more apartment complexes in the Las Vegas area, but since we were unable to verify their exact rates, they were not included in this list. There are many new ones that are in the process of being built and those, also, are unlisted in this directory at this time. There are some which offer specials such as half a month's free rent, microwaves, televisions, etc. Most complexes have swimming pools, jacuzzis and laundry facilities, and some have tennis courts, workout rooms, putting greens and outdoor barbecues. You would be wise to check on several to get the best deal.

Many people have inquired about how to rent a home or a condo. One source for leads would be the classified ads in the *Las Vegas Review Journal/Sun*. Another source would be real estate management companies. The following is a listing of some who advertise in the yellow pages that they handle home and condo rentals:

Century 21 Moneyworld
(702) 383-9886

Century 21 Moneyworld VIP Relocation
Nina Alioto
(702) 756-2121

Frasco Associates
(702) 892-3754

Help-U-Rent
(702) 253-7368

Insight Property Inc.
(702) 384-3153

Southwest Management Group
(702) 871-5177

Terra West
(702) 362-6262

    As in most cities, it will be far more difficult to find a home, condo, or apartment for rent if you have a pet. Be prepared to be "up front" with the people you are renting from. Tell them about your pet if you have one because not doing so could land you back on the street very quickly.

♥ ♣ ♦ ♠ ♥ ♣ ♦ ♠

HOMES IN LAS VEGAS

New home developments are popping up all over the Las Vegas area. There is every shape and style one could imagine, and the prices vary accordingly. To give you a few examples of pricing, the average home in a well-known area in southwest Las Vegas called Spanish Trails Country Club ranges from $200,000 to $600,000. There are also many custom homes on their golf course that range in price from one million dollars and up. One such home has over 15,000 square feet.

In other parts of our valley, there are many beautiful "custom" homes on half acres which can be had for $200,000 to $350,000. There are three-bedroom, two-bath homes in nice neighborhoods, with a pool, that are going for $125,000 to $175,000. And for the more economy minded, there are numerous three-bedroom, two-bath homes which can be had for $85,000 to $100,000. Often those are without a pool, but you might get lucky and find one in that price range with one.

There are many smaller homes on the market (1300-1400 sq. ft.), along with condominiums, townhouses and duplexes which are priced from $65,000 to $95,000.

People have been known to get a terrific deal in this town by shopping around. It always helps to have an astute real estate agent scouting out places for you too.

Many people find that buying a resale home, rather than a new one, is much to their advantage. Most of the resale homes already have mature landscaping, fences (block walls are very "in" out here), window coverings, and many have a pool or spa.

If one were to buy a new home, those items would all be additional expenses you would incur. You would probably be looking at a minimum of $10,000 more than the actual cost of the house. That, of course, does not include a pool or spa. A small pool (15' x 30') could cost anywhere from $12,000 and up, and 120 feet of block wall fencing would cost approximately $3000, unless you split that cost with your neighbor. Other costs incurred would be window coverings, which, if you had 12 windows and used very inexpensive mini-blinds, would end up costing between $1600 - $2000. Then there's the slab for the patio (12' x 12' would be about $400), and a patio cover, not to mention the landscaping or automatic sprinkler system. And then, of course, if you're not happy with the carpeting or flooring that the builder gives you, you will want to upgrade that, which could total thousands of dollars more.

When it comes to buying a home in Las Vegas, you get a lot for your money. An advertisement I read recently exemplifies that:

> For Sale: 4-bedroom, 2-bath home with 2-car garage, rock fireplace, pool with slide, built-in BBQ outside, mature landscaping with automatic sprinklers, highly upgraded new carpet and pad throughout. Entry, formal dining room and breakfast room with new wood floors. Breakfast Room has 6 French doors and ceiling fan/light. Home has formal dining room, living room, and family room. Over 2000 sq. ft. Professionally decorated with designer wall and window coverings. Beautiful one-story home - Must see. Close to schools and shopping. 8 minutes west of Strip. $135,000

I did see the house, and it had everything it said, plus a whole lot more. It was well worth $135,000. A couple from Southern California who toured the home said, "That same home in our area would sell for well over $350,000!" I guess that's why so many Californians are flocking to Las Vegas.

WHAT GOES AROUND, COMES AROUND

About three years ago, a local real estate agent stopped at a convenience store to buy a soda. As he was exiting the store, a young man who was in the parking lot asked his assistance. It seems he had a car problem and didn't have enough money to get the part to fix it. He asked the realtor if he would lend him $20. The realtor was somewhat skeptical, but felt the young man had a legitimate problem, so lent him the $20. The young man asked for his name and address and promised to repay the loan. The realtor gave him his business card. "My mother, and also a friend of hers, are moving here and want to look for houses," the boy said. "I'll send my mother your card and she'll call you." The realtor said, "Yes, have her do that," and all the while he was thinking, "Yes, a likely story!"

Two weeks later, the boy's mother called from California to say she was coming in and would like to go "house-hunting". Her friend called shortly thereafter, and also set an appointment with him. Not only did the realtor sell houses to both of them, but they had another friend they referred to him, and he sold a house to that lady too.

Not a bad return on a $20 kindness! And now I suppose you're going to ask, "Did the realtor ever get his $20 back from the young man?"

♥ ♣ ♦ ♠ ♥ ♣ ♦ ♠

NEW HOMES
AREAS AND PRICE RANGE

The following is a listing of new homes, condominiums and townhouses which have recently been built in the Las Vegas area. Wherever possible, we have tried to give you a price range. Most of the models are open seven days a week (average hours are 10:00 AM - 5:00 PM). If you are thinking of buying, it's a good idea to visit several while you are in Las Vegas on an inspection trip.

NORTHWEST
(West of Interstate 15/North of East Charleston)

DEVELOPMENT	PHONE	STARTING PRICE
Applause	254-8645	$95,000
Ascot Park	256-9842	$135,000
Belaire Estates	254-5451	$225,000
Belmont Terrace	399-8939	$95,000
Brentwood	228-3100	$129,000
Cascade	631-7134	$95,000
Cherry Creek	363-3596	$185,000
Churchill Estates	363-9323	$225,000
Collage	431-4477	$85,000
Coral Bay	255-4661	$139,000
Country Faire	259-8688	$95,000
Daybreak	646-2970	$95,000
Decatur Meadows	645-5616	$115,000
Deerbrooke	658-9398	$150,000
Desert Creek	658-5058	$85,000
Echo Bay Condominiums	457-0457	$69,000
Eldorado Ranch Homes	399-0533	$120,000
Eldorado Village Homes	399-5125	$89,000
Estancia	645-0779	$125,000
Evergreen	457-7373	$135,000
Executive Estates	645-4451	$200,000
Grand Entries	645-2936	$85,000
Harbor Point Executive Homes	228-1325	$189,000
Hidden Canyon	647-8751	$120,000
Indian Ridge	564-4035	$85,000
Isla Vista	254-3943	$115,000
Jamboree	656-8933	$110,000
La Mancha Townhomes	254-8303	$165,000

NORTHWEST (CONT')

DEVELOPMENT	PHONE	STARTING PRICE
La Posada Condominiums	254-4289	$55,000
La Quinta Springs	646-9381	$105,000
Las Hadas Townhomes	645-4412	$75,000
Los Prados	645-1562	$150,000
Marketplace	228-8308	$95,000
Montaire	254-2855	$155,000
Montaire Country Club Villas	254-2855	$140,000
Monte Vista	648-8800	$100,000
Mountain Shadows	645-3868	$139,000
Nevada Classic North	656-0855	$89,000
Norte del Sol	648-8667	$85,000
Pageantry Collection	646-5183	$95,000
Pageantry Fox Glen	645-7916	$149,000
Parkridge Homes	399-4149	$95,000
Pebble Canyon	897-2511	$95,000
Pizzaz	645-7990	$85,000
Plateau	254-8404	$95,000
Portraits	656-0609	$127,000
Rainbow Pointe	878-4501	$89,000
Rancho Alta Mira	656-8841	$100,000
Rancho Classic	646-6590	$79,000
Rancho Sierra	646-0599	$69,000
Reflection Series	256-1721	$115,000
Remington Homes	437-1057	$80,000
Ridgeview West	254-1722	$110,000
San Mateo Valley	658-8970	$85,000
Sandalwood	361-0191	$115,000
Scottsdale West Condominiums	645-6444	$75,000

NORTHWEST (CONT')

DEVELOPMENT	PHONE	STARTING PRICE
Sedona on the Park	255-8073	$149,000
Shadow Ridge	642-6030	$90,000
Sierra	631-3100	$85,000
Solana Del Norte	646-7967	$95,000
Sonterra	658-4501	$115,000
Silverado	228-5769	$85,000
Summer Breeze	656-7005	$95,000
Summerlin Information Center	791-4500	$100,000
Sunbeam	878-8500	$85,000
Sunset Ridge	631-4437	$98,000
Tahoe Executive Homes	254-1930	$169,000
Tiempo	645-6566	$95,000
Tierra Del Sol	658-2034	$105,000
Torrey Pines Village	647-1168	$79,000
Trophy	228-8305	$95,000
Uptown Estates III	645-1625	$95,000
Villa Pacifica Townhomes	367-8001	$115,000
The Village	648-1407	$75,000
Visions	256-9203	$125,000
Vista del Oro	254-3920	$115,000
Waterford Falls	254-6918	$165,000
Willowtree	254-2585	$135,000
Wind Chime	647-3065	$75,000
Winwood Ranch	648-3321	$115,000
Woodridge Estates	564-7833	$90,000

♥ ♣ ♦ ♠ ♥ ♣ ♦ ♠

NORTHEAST
(East of Interstate 15/North of East Charleston)

DEVELOPMENT	PHONE	STARTING PRICE
Autumn Place II	452-5074	$85,000
Hidden Desert	389-2157	$89,000
Morning Ridge	496-7828	$105,000
Remington Homes	437-1057	$79,000
Rosewalk	896-2990	$75,000
Skyline	644-8482	$85,000
Spring Terrace Townhomes	644-1917	$75,000
Sunrise	437-3700	$85,000
Sunrise Vista	438-4983	$115,000

♥ ♣ ♦ ♠ ♥ ♣ ♦ ♠

WEST
(West of Interstate 15 - Between Charleston & Tropicana)

DEVELOPMENT	PHONE	STARTING PRICE
All-American Homes	457-0062	$90,000
Cantera	228-2800	$125,000
Canyon Ridge at Peccole Ranch	363-8897	$195,000
Canyon Ridge, Series II	256-9870	$115,000
Classic Collection	363-1406	$160,000
Crystal Bay	254-8692	$190,000
Heritage Estates	225-1478	$210,000
Hillcrest Point	363-8141	$135,000
Orleans	364-1007	$120,000
Polo Greens	254-1154	$135,000
Rain Tree West Condominiums	227-4822	$69,000
South Point	363-1406	$110,000
Stone Canyon West	253-0111	$85,000
The Summit	363-7501	$160,000
Tahoe Executive Homes	254-1930	$169,000

♥ ♣ ♦ ♠ ♥ ♣ ♦ ♠

WEST / SOUTHWEST
(West of Interstate 15/South of Tropicana)

DEVELOPMENT	PHONE	STARTING PRICE
Las Verdes Condominiums	876-1201	$62,000
Norte del Sol	648-8667	$85,000
Orleans	364-1007	$125,000
Pebble Shores	496-3461	$92,000
Santa Margarita	258-0727	$75,000
Souvenir Homes	873-8553	$79,000
Sunflower	564-4035	$85,000
Tamarac	227-4838	$115,000
Villa Pacifica Townhomes	367-8001	$105,000
West Trop Condominiums	362-6280	$75,000
Westgate	367-3305	$145,000

♥ ♣ ♦ ♠ ♥ ♣ ♦ ♠

SOUTH / SOUTHEAST
(East of Interstate 15/South of Tropicana)

DEVELOPMENT	PHONE	STARTING PRICE
Allegro	896-3094	$120,000
Arbor Ridge	566-8502	$95,000
Autumn Place II	452-5074	$85,000
Avalon Village	361-7533	$95,000
Brookstone	361-0028	$125,000
Calypso	361-6025	$110,000
Canyon Willow	433-2021	$55,000
The Canyons	458-8684	$125,000
Celebrity II	432-3200	$125,000
Coral Ridge	595-5606	$125,000
Cortina	361-7060	$155,000
Delmonico	454-5313	$120,000
El Encanto	361-1679	$129,000
Encore Edition Townhomes	454-9713	$85,000
Environment for Living	896-8989	$115,000
The Gallery	361-1104	$220,000
Gold Dust Townhomes	739-7110	$95,000
Island Park	896-7055	$85,000
Jasmine Point	565-2900	$125,000
Legacy	896-1631	$115,000
Master Series	897-3520	$160,000
Monarch Ridge	458-1646	$185,000
Montelena	361-7610	$125,000
Paradise Vista	361-6059	$145,000
Pebble Canyon	897-0313	$99,000
Pebble Creek	897-4599	$95,000
The Reserve	896-9288	$189,000
Sandalwood	361-0191	$115,000
Serenade Condominiums	432-3202	$85,000
Shadow Canyon	434-9288	$129,000

SOUTH / SOUTHEAST (CONT')

DEVELOPMENT	PHONE	STARTING PRICE
Silver Mill	361-6630	$135,000
Summit Point	896-9288	$115,000
Sunset View	564-3609	$95,000
Vista del Oro	254-3920	$115,000
Windmill Villages	361-3477	$95,000

♥ ♣ ♦ ♠ ♥ ♣ ♦ ♠

EAST CENTRAL
(East of Las Vegas Blvd -
Between Charleston & Tropicana)

DEVELOPMENT	PHONE	STARTING PRICE
All-American Homes	457-0062	$90,000
Ascot Park	256-9842	$135,000
Collage	431-4477	$85,000
Echo Bay Condominiums	457-0457	$69,000
Pacific Montage	431-2508	$100,000
Peach Tree	431-8655	$95,000
Plum Tree	457-7373	$110,000
Summer Park	592-5450	$85,000
Topaz Court	892-9950	$115,000

♥ ♣ ♦ ♠ ♥ ♣ ♦ ♠

GETTING A MORTGAGE

The paperwork normally required to apply for most mortgages is as follows:

- Two years income tax returns
- Last three month's bank statements
- Verification of down payment
- Loan, credit card and bank account numbers
- Divorce papers, if divorced during the last three years
- DD214 and eligibility certificate for VA loans

A credit check will be done. The cost of this report, usually payable at the time you apply for the loan, is between $50 and $75. The lender will acquire an appraiser to appraise the property you wish to buy. The charge for that is between $250 - $350, depending upon the property. Normally, you are also required to pay for that at the time of loan application. At the close of escrow, you will encounter other fees, such as escrow fees, title fees, recording fees, documentation preparation charges, tax service fees, loan origination fees, and approximately 15 days of prepaid interest on the property. On an average $90,000 loan, you could expect to pay as much as $2000 in additional fees, in addition to your original down payment. The mortgage company will give you a Good Faith Estimate at the time you apply for the loan, showing an estimate of all fees.

There are various types of mortgages, depending on your personal financial situation. In addition to the standard 30-year mortgage, there are mortgages for 15 years, 7 years, and 5 years. The lesser the years, the better the interest rate you can acquire.

Some new home builders pick up most of the closing costs on a property if you buy from them, so if you are buying a new home rather than a resale home, check with the builder on what fees they will pay.

There are a few assumable, "no qualifying", properties available around the city, but those are becoming more scarce as the years roll on. However, a good real estate agent can usually find a few of them.

To give you a general idea of what your monthly mortgage payments would cost, we called Ms. Billie West at Nevada Federal Credit Union to give us an approximate breakdown. The following is what she gave us, saying these are only "ballpark figures", and do not include taxes or insurance. Your mortgage broker will give you exact figures when you apply for a loan.

MORTGAGE	APPROXIMATE MONTHLY PAYMENT			
	8.0%	8.5%	9.0%	9.5%
65,000	477.00	500.00	525.00	550.00
75,000	550.00	577.00	610.00	635.00
85,000	624.00	654.00	690.00	725.00
95,000	697.00	730.00	770.00	800.00
105,000	770.00	807.00	850.00	880.00
115,000	844.00	884.00	930.00	975.00
125,000	917.00	961.00	990.00	1050.00
135,000	991.00	1038.00	1020.00	1080.00
145,000	1064.00	1115.00	1170.00	1230.00
155,000	1137.00	1192.00	1248.00	1304.00
165,000	1211.00	1269.00	1328.00	1388.00

♥ ♣ ♦ ♠ ♥ ♣ ♦ ♠

A REAL ESTATE STORY
"THE FISH THAT GOT AWAY"

Approximately fourteen years ago, a close friend decided to go to real estate school. It was a major undertaking for someone who had been away from school, and studying, for eighteen years. She really applied herself. For the next six weeks, none of us saw her. She had her head buried in the books. When it was time to take the real estate test, she was a nervous wreck. She managed to pass with flying colors. That was not an easy task because about 50% of the people who took the test had to return and retake it. All her friends were very proud of her. We all tried our best to assist her in finding clients.

Shortly after she received her real estate license, she called to tell me about a land deal she had checked on. It seems there were ten-acre parcels available in the southeast desert for $3000 down and payments of $300 a month, with a total price of $30,000. It was what one would consider an investment for the future. I thought it sounded good, so I got on the phone and called six of my friends who, I felt, might be interested. A few of them were, and they bought. At that time, my husband and I had just bought a new home. We had invested everything we had. (After all, we absolutely had to have a pool installed, and of course we needed immediate landscaping!) We didn't have an extra $3000 available to put down on a pile of rocks in the desert.

Some of our friends who invested sold their ten-acre parcels about five or six years later, and more than doubled their investment. However, there were a few very wise friends who held on to their property. Today their ten-acre parcels, for which they paid a total of $30,000, are selling for $52,000 an acre. That's $520,000 for their 10-acre parcel.

I think we really didn't need a swimming pool during the first few months that we were in our new home. This incident - losing the opportunity to make a $490,000 profit - reinforces my belief in the old adage, "Business before pleasure!" It's unfortunate that we're so good at "hindsight" and so lax with "foresight". I hear this same type of story every day from a lot of the Las Vegas "old-timers" (people who've lived here twenty years or more). There were bargains to be had, but some of us weren't smart enough to get them!

♥ ♣ ♦ ♠ ♥ ♣ ♦ ♠

MOBILE HOME PARKS

There are well over 100 mobile home parks spread throughout the Las Vegas valley. At least ten of these are listed as "Adults Only". Space rent in mobile home parks has continued to climb over the past several years, and we are told that the average rent now runs between $350/month to $490/month. Some of the older parks and those parks which house only single-wide mobile homes charge a fair amount less than that. If you find a park that you are interested in, stop in at the office (usual office hours for most parks is 9:00 AM - 5:00 PM, Monday - Friday) to inquire about their rates and rules.

There are several mobile home companies in Las Vegas who sell both new and used homes. A used double-wide can range in price from $20,000 to $50,000, depending on the amenities. New double-wides start at $30,000 and go up from there. When buying a new one, you can usually negotiate with the dealer about delivery and set-up in the park of your choice. Some dealers include that with the price of the sale.

♥ ♣ ♦ ♠ ♥ ♣ ♦ ♠

UTILITIES

WHO?   WHERE?   HOW MUCH?

Let us proceed with the various utility companies. Since you cannot do without electricity, we will make that our first stop.

NEVADA POWER COMPANY

Main Office: 6226 West Sahara
8:00 AM - 8:00 PM

Branch Office: 3661 S. Maryland Pkwy
8:00 AM - 8:00 PM

You can make arrangements for the turn-on of your electricity at either of these locations. The phone number to call is the same for all branches: 367-5555. There are two additional branch offices to serve you if you are moving into Henderson/Green Valley or into North Las Vegas. Those addresses are:

227 Water Street
Henderson, NV
8:00 AM - 5:00 PM

1820 E. Lake Mead
North Las Vegas, NV
8:00 AM - 8:00 PM

The amount of deposit required, if any, is dependent upon your credit rating with the electric company you are presently using. If they will give you a letter of reference stating that you have been a credit-worthy customer, no deposit is required. If, however, you cannot obtain such a letter, you will be required to post a $50 - $90 deposit. The amount of deposit will again be dependent upon your overall credit rating. When applying for electricity, you must allow Nevada Power at least three working days to turn it on, although often it can be turned on in a day or two.

The average charge for electricity at the present time is approximately $.05 per kilowatt hour. You can make a cost comparison with your present electric company by checking your bill to see what they are charging per kilowatt hour. On your first month's bill you will also be charged a $7.50 connection fee.

♥ ♣ ♦ ♠ ♥ ♣ ♦ ♠

LAS VEGAS VALLEY WATER DISTRICT

Main Office: 3700 W. Charleston
               870-4194
               8:00 AM - 5:00 PM

Branch Office: 4160 South Pecos
               870-4194
               8:00 AM - 5:00 PM

If you are purchasing a home, no deposit is required. If you are renting a house, the deposit is $70. If renting a townhouse or condominium, the deposit is $40. Most generally, if you are renting an apartment, the cost of water is included in your rent, so a visit to the water company is not needed.

An average monthly bill of approximately $30 - $45 can be expected for a two-person home with a medium-sized lawn. That figure is based on the idea that both people take a daily shower, that the lawn needs daily watering, and that the couple use an automatic dishwasher, and also do approximately five to six loads of laundry per week. More people, more showers, and more loads of laundry would increase that figure somewhat.

Your monthly bill consists of a service charge, based on the size of your meter, and a charge for the amount of water used. Your threshold is 20,000 gallons per month (or 670 gallons per household day) for a 5/8" meter size. For use less than this threshold, you will pay .98 per thousand gallons of water. If you use more, you will pay $1.16 per thousand gallons for the water you use above your 20,000 gallons per month threshold limit.

To conserve water, desert landscaping is encouraged when buying a home. At the present time, Las Vegas has enough water to supply our ever-growing region. The Water District wishes to ensure the long-term supply. To do that, they have begun an increased cost (or penalty) on those households which use excessive amounts each month.

The following is a list of water rate comparisons by city for use of 22.2 thousand gallons of water per month using information supplied by the Las Vegas Valley Water District (January 1992).

Santa Barbara, CA	155.62
Houston, TX	73.01
Colorado Springs, CO	43.90
Oakland, CA	43.18
Scottsdale, AZ	37.27

Dallas, TX	36.33
Los Angeles, CA	35.68
San Diego, CA	29.17
Phoenix, AZ	28.46
Oklahoma City, OK	27.90
Las Vegas, NV	25.49

♥ ♣ ♦ ♠ ♥ ♣ ♦ ♠

SOUTHWEST GAS COMPANY

Main Office: 4300 W. Tropicana
               365-1555
               8:00 AM - 5:00 PM

Branch Office: 2107 Civic Center
               North Las Vegas, NV
               365-1555
               8:00 AM - 5:00 PM

You can make arrangements via telephone to have the gas connected if you have the necessary credit information available. They will want your name, address, phone number, social security number, personal references, and your present and previous places of employment for both you and your spouse, if applicable. They require a $50 deposit. If you bring a letter of reference from the gas company you previously used showing that you are credit-worthy, they will forego the deposit. There will be a $20 connection charge on your first month's billing. You must allow approximately three days for your service to be connected.

On the day that your connection is scheduled, someone must be present at the home or apartment from 8:00 AM until 6:00 PM to allow the serviceman entry. If he arrives and no one is there, you must call to reschedule the hook-up. It is imperative that both the electricity and the water are connected before the gas. If this is not done, again you will have to reschedule with the gas company once the other two utilities are connected. If you want your gas connected on the same day that you apply for it, the connection charge is $40.

* * * * * * *

It is difficult to judge exactly what your gas and electric bills will be. Often times you have gas heat for the winter and electric for your air conditioner in the summer. Then again, some homes are all electric. My husband and I lived in a 2000 sq. ft., all-electric home until three years ago. We had a pool (which needed electricity for the pool motor), laundry facilities, a dishwasher, furnace, and air conditioner, and of course, a water heater and daily lights. During March - May and September - November, our monthly electric bill averaged $85. During the summer and in the winter, our electric bill averaged $125. I might add, our home was well-insulated and had thermo-pane windows which are a great help in keeping the heat and cold out. That was three years ago and rates have increased somewhat since then.

A very reputable building contractor in this city informed me that if you have the dual-pane windows in your home, along with roof exhaust fans to take the heat out of the attic in the summer, and three-foot roof overhangs, you can save a fair amount on your energy costs. The next step is to find an "energy conscious" builder.

♥ ♣ ♦ ♠ ♥ ♣ ♦ ♠

CENTEL PHONE SERVICE

330 South Valley View
Residential Service: 877-7400
Business Service: 877-7711

Office Hours: 8:00 AM - 6:00 PM,
                Monday - Friday
                9:00 AM - 1:00 PM,
                Saturday

Branch Offices: Renaissance Office
                East Tropicana/Eastern

                North Las Vegas Office
                Lake Mead/Civic Center

                Henderson Office
                104 Water Street

Telephone service can be arranged from your home state by calling 1-800-877-7077. You will need to give several credit references. If you presently have telephone service in your home state, and have maintained an excellent credit rating with them, no deposit will be required. If you have not had previous telephone service in your name, the required deposit will depend on your credit rating. If your credit rating is less than perfect, the minimum deposit you will be required to post is $50. It could be more than that if your credit rating shows you as a "slow pay", and a whole lot more if the report shows even one "no pay".

When making arrangements for your telephone installation, you must advise Centel which long distance service you wish to use. These include the following:

COMPANY	RESIDENTIAL	BUSINESS
A T & T	800-222-0300	800-222-0400
Access Long Distance	702-383-0030	702-385-3311
American Network Exchange		800-366-2850
CRC Corporation	702-366-9111	702-366-9111
Cable & Wireless	800-486-8686	800-486-8686
Com Systems, Inc.	702-873-8841	702-873-8841
Express Tel		702-731-2776
Long Distance for Less	702-387-1113	702-387-1113
MCI Telecommunications	800-444-7373	

COMPANY	RESIDENTIAL	BUSINESS
Metromedia ITT		800-275-2273
Tel Com International		702-641-5177
Telecom USA/Teleconnect	800-728-7000	800-728-7000
US Sprint	800-877-4646	800-877-4646

It will be your responsibility to call any one of these long distance services to advise them that you wish to use their service. You will need to advise them of the new phone number you will have, and allow them up to a week to place the service on your line.

When ordering your phone service from Centel, you should allow approximately five days for them to install. However, sometimes they can install within a day or two. It all depends on how busy they are. We do have a large influx of people moving to Las Vegas every month, and often the Centel offices are inundated with orders. Most generally, the installation is done promptly with few delays. The minimum installation charge is $18.75 plus tax, and will appear on your first month's billing. The installation charge could run higher if you run additional phone lines or have extra phone jacks installed. The residential phone charge for one line is approximately $12.50 with taxes. The average monthly cost for a business line is approximately $24.00 per line when you include the federal subscriber line charge and tax.

♥ ♣ ♦ ♠ ♥ ♣ ♦ ♠

SILVER STATE DISPOSAL

770 E. Sahara
735-5151
Office Hours: 8:00 AM - 5:00 PM

Anyone buying a home must contract with Silver State Disposal to pick up their garbage twice weekly. If renting a house, condominium, townhouse, or apartment, that service is usually included with your rent. If it is not, or if you are buying a home, the "quarterly" cost is $27.00, which averages out to $9.00 per month.

♥ ♣ ♦ ♠ ♥ ♣ ♦ ♠

CABLE TELEVISION

Now that we have you comfortably situated with your necessary utilities, you may want to indulge yourself with cable television. If so, the following is a list of cable services in our community. It is up to you which one you wish to choose. However, not all of them service every neighborhood.

Clover Cable	733-8508
Empire Cable	293-2133
Interface Communications	876-3474
JR's Cable Service	798-2999
M C Communications	367-1103
MISCO, Inc.	361-8621
Nellis Cable	644-2400
Prime Cable of Las Vegas	383-4000

There is usually an installation charge in addition to the monthly service you request. Your monthly service could run from approximately $27 for basic service up to $80 for full service, getting every channel.

♥ ♣ ♦ ♠ ♥ ♣ ♦ ♠

DEPARTMENT OF MOTOR VEHICLES

The grace period for obtaining a Nevada driver's license and plates upon becoming a resident is 45 days.

DRIVER'S LICENSE

To acquire a Nevada driver's license, you must produce proof of your social security number via a social security card, W-2 form, printed payroll check with your name and number, or an old income tax return. You must surrender your out-of-state license and take both a written test and a vision test. It is wise to acquire a Nevada driver's handbook to read and study a few days before the written test. Some of the questions can be tricky. Even the wisest of us can sometimes be fooled. The cost for the license is $20. If you are age 65 or over, the charge is $10. Your driver's license is good for four years and expires on your birthday. There is also a service available at the Department of Motor Vehicles for persons who do not drive to acquire a photo I.D. The cost is also $10.

NEVADA LICENSE PLATES

Your new plates may be acquired at either of these two locations:

2701 E. Sahara   7:30 AM - 5:00 PM, M-F
4021 W. Carey   8:00 AM - 5:00 PM, M-F

You must present the following documentation upon registering your vehicle:

1. Your title of ownership (unless it is being held by a lienholder)
2. Your most recent registration
3. A Nevada Smog Inspection Certificate
4. A Nevada-approved insurance card from a Nevada-licensed insurance agent
5. Your out-of-state plates
6. A vehicle inspection certificate
7. A reading of your odometer
8. Copy of lease agreement if leased vehicle

The cost for registering your vehicle and acquiring your Nevada License plates varies according to the make and model of your car. To give you an idea of the variation, a friend registered her 1991 Oldsmobile 88 (fully loaded) and her costs were $290. Another registered her 1987 Nissan Maxima and paid $150. The smaller and older the car, the less the cost. There are no additional fees, such as a "city sticker", which some cities require.

For further vehicle registration information, you may call (702) 641-0090. There is also further information provided via recorded messages by dialing (702) 486-4368.

There are additional express offices for the Department of Motor Vehicles. However, these are for renewing driver's licenses or vehicle registrations. They do not give driver's tests or issue new plates at those locations.

When going to register your vehicle and get new license plates, you may spend hours in line waiting. I came across a service that will do it for you if you are not into wasting time standing in line. It's called V.I.P. Services. Their phone number is 361-8387. They charge $30.00 to take this hassle out of your life. A lot of the "very busy" business people take advantage of the service.

♥ ♣ ♦ ♠ ♥ ♣ ♦ ♠

In summarizing the basic relocation costs, we'll pretend that you have arrived in Las Vegas and have found a house to rent. An average rental for an average three-bedroom house would be approximately $700 - $1200 per month. Using the hypothetical rental figure of $850, we'll construct a cost chart for you, pretending that you must give full deposits to each utility.

INITIAL ESTIMATED EXPENSES

First Month's Rent	$850.00
Security Deposit	$850.00
Nevada Power Deposit	$90.00
Water District Deposit	$70.00
Gas Deposit	$50.00
Centel Phone Service	$50.00
Driver's License	$20.00
Nevada License Plates (Mid-size 1991 vehicle)	$250.00
TOTAL DEPOSITS	**$2230.00**

FIRST MONTH'S ESTIMATED EXPENSES

Electric Service	
Installation Charge ($7.50)	$ 55.00
Gas Service	
Installation Charge ($20)	$100.00
Water Service	$15.00
Telephone	
Installation Charge ($18.75)	$38.75
Silver State Disposal (1st Quarter)	$24.63
Basic Cable Service	$28.00
Four Weeks of Groceries (for two)	$145.00
Four Weeks of Gasoline for your car	$80.00
Miscellaneous Expenses	$300.00
TOTAL EXPENSES	**$786.38**

The total amount for deposits and expenses for the first month equals $3016.38. And don't forget to continue your payments for your health, life and car insurance.

Your second month's bills should be considerably less because you won't be paying a rental security deposit or utility deposits and installation charges. Using this chart, you could possibly figure your second month's total expenses to be around $1670 for two people.

This was an average for middle class living. Your overall expenses could be considerably less expensive. In the area of rents, there are apartments for rent in the range of $400 - $500 which also require a smaller security deposit. Then, if you have excellent credit, you would forego various utility deposits, and if you have a small economy car, your license plates would cost less, as would the amount of gas you use to get around town. AND, if you're a light eater or a coupon shopper, you could cut that grocery bill in half too.

Automobile insurance and gas for your car seem to run higher than in the vast majority of cities. A friend who owns a 1993 Mercury Sable pays $590 every six months for insurance. Since he hasn't had any accidents or tickets for bad driving in over five years, this $590 includes his "safe-driver" discounts. He has full coverage on his car with a $250 deductible.

♥ ♣ ♦ ♠ ♥ ♣ ♦ ♠

YOUR PERSONAL COST WORKSHEET FOR MOVING TO LAS VEGAS

Moving Van Charges From Your City	$_____
Air Fare If Flying	$_____
Gas for Car, If Driving to Las Vegas	$_____
Motel Costs En Route	$_____
Food Costs En Route	$_____
Motel Costs Upon Arrival	$_____
Housing Deposits	
First Month's Rent/Mortgage	$_____
Last Month's Rent	$_____
Cleaning Fee on Rental	$_____
Security Deposit on Rental	$_____

Utility Deposits

    Electricity $____

    Telephone $____

    Gas $____

    Water $____

    Garbage Pick-Up (If Buying) $____

    Cable Television $____

    Sanitation (If Buying) $____

Car Registration (NV License Plates) $____

Nevada Driver's License ($20 each) $____

One Month's Car Insurance $____

One Month's Grocery Expense $____

One Month's Supply of Gasoline $____

Additional Miscellaneous Expenses $____

TOTAL EXPENSES $____

Now is the time to start saving for that "Total Expenses" amount. Moving to Las Vegas with less than that is not wise. Nevada is not known to be a welfare state. It is very difficult, and a long drawn-out process, to acquire any kind of welfare benefits. You could get pretty hungry waiting for them.

♥ ♣ ♦ ♠ ♥ ♣ ♦ ♠

A PROPER WELCOME TO LAS VEGAS

When Carol, from Chicago, turned 21, her goal was to travel to Las Vegas and become a blackjack dealer. About six months after her 21st birthday, she flew to Las Vegas. She moved in with her father and his wife, and began attending dealer's school.

When Thanksgiving rolled around, her stepmother began cooking a big Thanksgiving dinner. Grandma was visiting and was trying to be helpful in the small kitchen, but she was getting underfoot. A plea was whispered to Carol - "Please do me a favor. Take my mother out for an hour of bingo so I can get this dinner fixed." Carol agreed, and off they went. Two hours later, they returned, all smiles. Carol had won $1000 on the "cover-all" at bingo. The next day found Carol at a used car lot buying her first car.

Just a few months later, Carol made a date to meet friends for something to eat at a local casino. Carol's work shift ended an hour earlier than expected, so she went to the casino. She decided to play bingo while she waited for her friends to arrive. By the time they did, she was bursting with excitement. She had just won another $1000. This time, she went to buy furniture for the new condominium she was about to buy.

Nine years later, Carol insists that she has donated back to the bingo parlor more than the original $2000 she had won. Those original winnings gave her a running start in Las Vegas. After she had lived here for less than two years, she had a nice used car that was paid for, new furniture, and a nice little condominium of her own that she had saved for. Not bad for a girl who was only 22 years old at the time. Today, she is married, has a child, and is a casino executive at a prominent hotel/casino.

****

You hear a lot about "winning" and "losing" in Las Vegas, but there's another thing that the vast majority of Las Vegas residents do. It's called "saving". How else could our construction industry continue to build thousands of new homes throughout the city? If the people hadn't saved their money to buy a new home, the overwhelming demand wouldn't be there. As it is now, every direction out from the heart of the city is teeming with new housing.

The gambling industry has created thousands of jobs for Las Vegas residents, and most of them give a "little" bit back every year by putting some coins in a slot machine, playing bingo, or betting on a football game. It's when you find that you are giving your whole paycheck back that you had better think of moving to another city, because obviously you have a problem. Of course, there is an organization called Gamblers Anonymous that could help. It reminds me of the story of the man who moved to Las Vegas who was a "multi-millionaire". Now he's a "millionaire".

♥ ♣ ♦ ♠ ♥ ♣ ♦ ♠

EMPLOYMENT

Now that we have you situated with your living arrangements, utilities, driver's license and vehicle registration, it is time to get a job. That is, if you haven't moved here to retire or to open your own business.

New companies opening in Las Vegas have provided many new jobs in all areas. During the past year, the strongest growth in the job markets was shown to be in gaming and hotels, housing, medical, service businesses, retail trade, and construction.

For persons looking for a part-time job, there is a host of fast food restaurants and convenience stores that constantly advertise for "help wanted". There are also many openings for newspaper delivery people and telephone sales. There are numerous temporary employment services who supply businesses with temporary employees. A complete listing of these agencies can be found in the telephone book yellow pages under "Employment - Temporary". There is usually no fee to the employee since most temporary agencies bill the employer directly.

It is a very good idea to start your search for a full-time job with a professionally prepared resume in your hand. Employers tend to look more favorably at the applicant who has made the effort to do this. Oftentimes, a good source for finding a job is the "Employment Opportunities" listing in the classified section of the Sunday *Las Vegas Review Journal/Sun* newspaper. Many companies, including many of the hotels, list job openings there.

The state-run agency which sends prospective employees for interviews is Nevada Employment Security. They have three employment offices:

135 S. 8th Street / 486-3300
2827 Las Vegas Blvd. North / 486-5600
119 S. Water St., Henderson / 486-6710

Upon arrival at any of these offices, check the bulletin board where all jobs are posted. They list the job title, duties, salary and hours. The name or phone number of the company soliciting for employees will not be listed. You must meet with a Nevada Employment Security counselor to acquire this information. You may request to be sent for interviews on the jobs you feel you are qualified for. There is no charge for this service since it is a state agency.

If you are seeking a job associated with the hospitality/hotel industry, go to the individual hotel personnel offices and check their bulletin boards. Many of them have their hotel job openings posted there.

If you have a specific trade that is covered by a union, it would be wise to go to that particular union. Register with them as soon as you arrive in Las Vegas. Since you are a newcomer, your name will undoubtedly be placed at the bottom of the list. That is why it's a good idea to register with them immediately. There are people registering daily, so the sooner you apply, the sooner your name moves up the list. The following is a list of the various labor unions who can help you:

AMERICAN POSTAL WORKERS
    1641 E. Sunset
    Las Vegas, NV 89119
    (702) 361-2798

BARTENDERS & BEVERAGE LOCAL 165
    1819 Industrial Road
    Las Vegas, NV 89102
    (702) 384-7774

BRICKLAYERS & TILE SETTERS LOCAL 3
4200 E. Bonanza
Las Vegas, NV   89110
(702) 452-8699

CARPENTERS LOCAL 1780
501 N. Lamb
Las Vegas, NV   89110
(702) 453-2206

CENTRAL LABOR COUNCIL - COPE
4200 E. Bonanza
Las Vegas, NV   89110
(702) 452-8799

CLARK COUNTY PUBLIC EMPLOYEES LOCAL 1107
1250 Burnham
Las Vegas, NV   89104
(702) 386-8849

CULINARY WORKERS LOCAL 226
1630 S. Commerce
Las Vegas, NV   89102
(702) 385-2131

FLOOR COVERINGS, GLAZIERS, & ALLIED TRADES - LOCAL 2001
    3432 Bruce
    Las Vegas, NV   89119
    (702) 399-4555

INTERNATIONAL ASSOCIATION OF FIREFIGHTERS LOCAL 1285
    3021 E. Charleston Blvd.
    Las Vegas, NV   89104
    (702) 383-9880

INTERNATIONAL ASSOCIATION OF FIREFIGHTERS LOCAL 1908
    5650 W. Charleston
    Las Vegas, NV   89102
    (702) 870-1908

INTERNATIONAL ASSOCIATION OF MACHINISTS LOCAL 845
    501 N. Lamb
    Las Vegas, NV   89110
    (702) 452-4699

INTERNATIONAL BROTHERHOOD OF ELECTRICAL WORKERS LOCAL 357
    4321 E. Bonanza
    Las Vegas, NV   89110
    (702) 452-9357

INTERNATIONAL BROTHERHOOD OF ELECTRICAL WORKERS LOCAL 396
3520 Boulder Highway
Las Vegas, NV   89121
(702) 457-3011

INTERNATIONAL HODCARRIERS BUILDING & COMMON LABORERS LOCAL 872
4200 E. Bonanza
Las Vegas, NV   89110
(702) 452-4440

INTERNATIONAL UNION OF OPERATING ENGINEERS LOCAL 12
360 Shadow Lane
Las Vegas, NV   89106
(702) 598-1212

INTERNATIONAL UNION OF OPERATING ENGINEERS LOCAL 501
301 Deauville Drive
Las Vegas, NV   89106
(702) 382-8452

IRON WORKERS LOCAL 433
4000 Boulder Highway
Las Vegas, NV   89121
(702) 456-1161

LAUNDRY & DRY CLEANERS LOCAL 311
    1311 S. Casino Center
    Las Vegas, NV   89104
    (702) 382-4919

MILLWRIGHTS LOCAL 1827
    501 N. Lamb
    Las Vegas, NV   89110
    (702) 452-8998

MUSICIANS LOCAL 369
    155 E. Tropicana
    Las Vegas, NV   89109
    (702) 739-9369

NATIONAL MARITIME UNION OF AMERICAN AFL-CIO
    720 E. Charleston
    Las Vegas, NV   89104
    (702) 384-7171

NEVADA STATE AFL-CIO COPE
    4200 E. Bonanza
    Las Vegas, NV   89110
    (702) 452-8799

PAINTERS LOCAL 159
501 N. Lamb
Las Vegas, NV   89110
(702) 452-2140

PLASTERERS & CEMENT MASONS LOCAL 797
4200 E. Bonanza
Las Vegas, NV   89110
(702) 452-9199

PLUMBERS & PIPEFITTERS LOCAL 525
735 N. Lamb
Las Vegas, NV   89110
(702) 452-1520

ROCKY MOUNTAIN WORK PROJECT AFL-CIO
4200 E. Bonanza
Las Vegas, NV   89110
(702) 459-1414

ROOFERS LOCAL 162
4200 E. Bonanza
Las Vegas, NV   89110
(702) 453-5801

SCREEN ACTORS GUILD OF NEVADA
3305 W. Spring Mountain, #60
Las Vegas, NV   89102
(702) 367-8217

SHEET METAL LOCAL 88
501 N. Lamb
Las Vegas, NV   89110
(702) 452-4799

SOUTHERN NEVADA OPERATING ENGINEERS, JOURNEYMAN
2750 E. Ann Road
Las Vegas, NV   89115
(702) 649-7888

SOUTHERN NEVADA OPERATION & MAINTENANCE ENGINEERS
313 Deauville Drive
Las Vegas, NV   89106
(702) 385-5005

TEAMSTERS LOCAL 14
303 Wall
Las Vegas, NV   89102
(702) 384-7841

TEAMSTERS LOCAL 995
300 Shadow Lane
Las Vegas, NV   89106
(702) 385-0995

TEAMSTERS & TRUCK DRIVERS LOCAL 631
307 Wall Street
Las Vegas, NV   89102
(702) 385-1455

THEATRICAL EMPLOYEES I.A.T.S.E. LOCAL 720
3000 S. Valley View
Las Vegas, NV   89102
(702) 873-3450

UNITED BROTHERHOOD OF BOILERMAKERS, RIGGERS, WELDERS, FITTERS, HELPERS UNION
1919 E. Hallwood Drive
Las Vegas, NV   89119
(702) 798-7245

UNITED FOOD & COMMERCIAL WORKERS UNION LOCAL 711
1201 N. Decatur
Las Vegas, NV   89108
(702) 648-1400

UNITED STEEL WORKERS OF AMERICA LOCAL 4856
47 S. Water Street
Henderson, NV   89014
(702) 565-8207

♥ ♣ ♦ ♠ ♥ ♣ ♦ ♠

If you obtain a job where food or beverage handling is necessary, or child care is involved, you must go to the Clark County Health District to obtain a health card. You must have a health card in your possession at all times when handling food or beverages for the public, or working in the child care field. This card may be obtained at the Health District office located at 625 Shadow Lane. You will be required to watch a movie on food and beverage handling before you receive your card. The present cost of the card is $10. For further information on health cards, contact the Clark County Health District at (702) 383-1226.

If you obtain a job where liquor is sold, you will also be required to have a Sheriff's Work Card and an Awareness Card. You do not obtain those until you have actually been hired. At that time, your employer will give you the necessary forms to take to those two divisions to obtain your cards.

The cost of the Sheriff's Work Card is $12, and can be obtained at 601 East Fremont (directly across the street from the El Cortez Hotel) between the hours of 8:00 AM and 4:00 PM, Monday through Friday. Do plan to stand in line for a short time as they are usually quite busy, and be sure to have identification, along with the necessary form from your employer.

Although you personally may not be handling or selling liquor, if it is sold on the premises you may be required to have an alcohol Awareness Card. This is obtained by attending a class on alcohol awareness. The cost of the class is $25. In some instances, your employer may pay for you to attend the class. The class is conducted at various locations, but your employer will give you a slip telling you which one you must attend. Again, be sure to take the employer slip with you, along with identification. The class lasts about four hours.

♥ ♣ ♦ ♠ ♥ ♣ ♦ ♠

AREAS OF JOB EXPERTISE NEEDED

In speaking with a prominent building contractor, I was informed of areas of employment associated with the housing industry where he feels there is a need for additional, highly-skilled individuals. Since there are so many people buying new homes, the demand for professional carpet layers and flooring installers is at an all-time high, as is the need for experienced interior decorators, custom drapery makers and installers, wallcovering installers, upholsterers, and cabinet makers. These are specialized areas where a dependable, highly talented individual could excel and do very well. Builders of swimming pools seem to be overloaded with work because most home buyers end up wanting a pool for those warm summer days, or a jacuzzi for those comfortable winter nights.

There seems to be job openings in virtually every phase of the medical community. Training in that field could land a good job for you.

Nevada Business Services at 930 West Owens assists "displaced workers" who have been laid off and cannot find another job in their area of previous experience. Their phone number is (702) 384-7655. They help locate jobs and often provide new job training also.

Many of the food service jobs in the hotels are obtained through the Culinary Union, as are many of the housekeeping jobs. A lot of the front desk positions and back office support people are hired through the Teamsters Union. There are, however, many restaurants and smaller hotel properties that do their own hiring without the unions.

Another profession in high demand is the mechanic. Every mechanic's shop in the city which has highly-skilled mechanics is always filled to capacity with cars to be worked on. It has been our experience that the very good shops require an appointment as much as a week in advance because they are so busy.

Although Las Vegas is growing by leaps and bounds, in its own way, it is still a small town. If a business is good, whether it be a mechanic's shop or a restaurant, the word gets around quickly. However, the same is true if the business does not handle their customers courteously and fairly. Because the townspeople are generally a friendly and helpful group, they tend to talk to strangers and recommend to them a business where they have been treated well. They also tend to discourage people from going to places where the service is less than professional and the workers are rude and arrogant. Many businesses have gone under for those very reasons. If you are planning to open a business in Las Vegas, remember that! There is a lot of competition out there and those who give excellent service, have pleasant employees, and provide quality merchandise at reasonable prices seem to excel.

♥ ♣ ♦ ♠ ♥ ♣ ♦ ♠

THE EMPLOYMENT AGENCY

All employment agencies are governed by the Nevada State Labor Commission. The fees charged are regulated by the Commission. Many employers do not wish to advertise in the newspapers for the jobs they have available. They become inundated with phone calls and must spend countless hours interviewing unqualified applicants. That is why some employers give their job listings to an employment agency. It is the agency's duty to have the applicants fill out an application, at which time the agency interviews and screens them. It is only after checking each applicant's references and verifying that they may be qualified for the position offered that the employment agency sets an appointment with the employer. All reputable agencies follow these procedures because they do not want to waste the time of either the employer or the applicant. Numerous executive positions are cycled through an employment agency rather than being advertised in the newspapers.

Some employers pay the employment fee to the agencies, while other employers split the fee with the person they hire. However, there are some jobs offered that require the employee to pay the fee in full. The fee is normally 65% of your first month's gross salary. That may seem high to some people, but more often than not, it is worth it in the long run.

♥ ♣ ♦ ♠ ♥ ♣ ♦ ♠

CASINO JOBS

The expected wages of a "dealing" job in the gaming industry run pretty close to minimum wage. It is the "tokes" (sometimes referred to as "tips") on which the dealers live. The tokes can average anywhere from $20 a day to $150. Those figures are contingent on which casino you are employed at, what season it is, and other variables. The $150 a day in tokes is somewhat unusual on a daily basis. It is probably more common at a hotel/casino on New Year's Eve. The average that most dealers earn in tokes is probably more in the category of $50 - $60 a day. If you add that to a salary of about $30 a day, you're ending up with about $400 - $450 a week. There are some hotels where the tokes are better than that. However, there are waiting lists of experienced dealers for them. At one such hotel, there was a day in 1991 where the dealers each made $1400 in tokes for the day. And the following day, they made several hundred more. Those are the kind of days that dreams are made of!

****

Another story, widely circulated among casino personnel, was that of a fortunate cocktail waitress who was in the right place at the right time. There was a very "high roller" playing in the hotel where she worked. During the previous year, she had waited on him several times. This time he recognized her as she served the table where he was playing. She greeted him by name, and he asked, "Are you still working here?" She answered, "Of course. I have a mortgage to pay off!" He then said, "How much is your mortgage?" She told him, and he proceeded to pick up that many thousand dollar chips in front of him and place them on her cocktail tray. "Here," he said. "Go pay off your mortgage!"

It was probably one of the largest tips ever paid to one individual in Las Vegas because the balance on her mortgage was no "small potatoes". Many people who knew the waitress agreed that this type of luck could not have happened to a nicer, or more hard-working person.

There are more stories out there about big tips and good luck, and maybe one day we'll be telling <u>your</u> story.

****

Most hotel/casinos offer hospitalization to their employees after they have been employed, full-time, for three months. Some casinos offer the hospitalization after six months, and some offer it after just thirty days.

When you apply for a job as a dealer, you are usually expected to pass an audition. That is where you deal to the casino's customers for approximately a half hour, under the watchful eye of one or more of the casino executives. Should you pass the audition, the average waiting time before you are hired can be from one to two weeks. Oftentimes, you will be started on the "extra board". You will eventually work full-time, but in the interim, you will be "on call". Usually, the casino guarantees you "X" amount of hours per week on the extra board. Yes, it takes patience and cooperation to break in to dealing. By the looks of the beautiful homes they live in, and the nice cars many of the casino personnel drive, I would say that in most cases, it all becomes worth it.

If you are planning to become a dealer, you must also plan to stand on your feet for approximately seven hours a day. This type of job requires a very good pair of comfortable shoes (sneakers not allowed). Several dealers who I spoke with told me of some wonderful new insoles that make walking and standing a pleasure. It seems that the innovative store, "Sharper Image", came up with some water-filled insoles that almost massage your feet while wearing them. They said the cost for these particular insoles is more than others, but it's worth it if you have a job where you are on your feet for long periods of time. This is just one of the gems of information I picked up while interviewing casino employees.

    The complaints about "dealing jobs" that I heard most from the dealers were: 1) Drunk and obnoxious customers who are at your table for hours. You cannot walk away and you must be nice to them. 2) People constantly blowing smoke in your face. 3) The odd hours (and holidays) you sometimes have to work, which can disrupt your social and family life. They all agree it's a great job for meeting people from all over the world. The overall majority seemed pleased with the profession they have chosen. One happy-go-lucky dealer put it very well. He said, "It's like going to a party to play games.....every day!"

♥ ♣ ♦ ♠ ♥ ♣ ♦ ♠

AVERAGE SALARIES

With the cost of living being less than in other metropolitan areas, some salaries also tend to be less. The salaries here, on an average, do cover your living expenses quite nicely, unless, of course, you happen to be a habitual gambler. In that case, chances are, whatever you earn won't be enough! The following are average "beginning" salaries, not including any tips or commissions.

Bank Teller	$6.50/Hour
Bellman	$44.14/Shift
Bookkeeper	$8-$11/Hour
Bus Driver (First 6 months)	$7/Hour
Car Valet	$5/Hour ++
Casino Dealer	$35/Day ++
Casino Floorman	$85-$175/Shift
Casino Security Guard	$6/Hour and up
Day Care Center Attendant	$7-$10/Hour
Dining Room Hostess	$66.68/Shift
Electrician	$23.13/Hour
Executive Secretary	$10/Hour
Finish Carpenter - Apprentice	$10-18/Hour
- Journeyman	$26.66/Hour

Grocery Store Checker - Apprentice	$6.60/Hour
Hotel Front Desk (First 6 mos)	$8/Hour
Hotel Reservationist (First 6 months)	$8/Hour
Hotel Sales Representative	$25,000 - $30,000/Year
Interior Decorator	$25/Hour
Maid	$56.02/Shift
Mechanic	$12/Hour
Painter - Apprentice	$8.62/Hour
Paralegal	$10/Hour
Plumber - Journeyman	$24.30/Hour
Registered Nurse	$22-$31/Hour
Retail Sales Clerk	$5/Hour +
Secretary	$8/Hour
Teacher (First Year)	$21,750/Year
Waiter/Waitress	$44.42/Shift

Taxi and limousine drivers, real estate sales people, and insurance agents, as well as numerous other sales jobs, are paid by commission percentage only. Taking a job in those fields can be very lucrative if you are knowledgeable, personable, and have a good sense of self-confidence.

TRADE SCHOOLS

Many people move here with the idea that they will get into the gaming industry. The casinos do not hire you just because you look nice. You must have training or experience in the gaming field to acquire a job here. If you do not have previous experience, the place to start is at a local gaming school. They teach blackjack, craps, baccarat, poker, roulette, paigow, and paigow poker. If you are mechanically or electronically inclined, you may choose to go to a school to learn to become a slot machine technician. Most of these schools offer day and evening classes and assistance in job placement. Many of them are approved for VA benefits or offer a payment plan.

The costs for the classes vary from school to school, but to give you a general idea, one of the major schools that we checked quoted the following costs for each of the various classes:

Craps	$295
Blackjack	$225
Roulette	$195
Paigow or Paigow Poker	$195
Baccarat	$195

The average length of an individual class could run from four to six weeks. If you have difficulty learning, they will allow you to stay on longer until you master the game. Several of the schools associate themselves with one particular casino where they will eventually take you for "live" training. Also, if you decide to take more than one class, you are usually given a good discount on the additional classes. The following is a listing of some of the gaming schools which are advertised in the telephone book yellow pages:

A-PCI
    920 S. Valley View
    Las Vegas, NV   89107
    (702) 877-4724

CASINO DEALERS SCHOOL
    1126 Fremont Street
    Las Vegas, NV   89101
    (702) 733-0400

DEALING SCHOOL A-ACTIVE
    557 E. Sahara Avenue
    Las Vegas, NV   89104
    (702) 732-0122

FREMONT STREET DEALERS SCHOOL
    503 E. Fremont
    Las Vegas, NV   89101
    (702) 387-1360

INTERNATIONAL DEALERS SCHOOL
    1030 E. Twain
    Las Vegas, NV   89109
    (702) 733-9133

INTERNATIONAL DEALERS SCHOOL
    1111 Las Vegas Blvd. South
    Las Vegas, NV   89104
    (702) 385-7665

INTERNATIONAL DEALERS SCHOOL
    2309 Las Vegas Blvd. South
    Las Vegas, NV   89104
    (702) 734-7222

LAS VEGAS GAMING & TECHNICAL
    3030 S. Highland
    Las Vegas, NV   89109
    (702) 733-3030

LAS VEGAS SCHOOL OF DEALING
    3850 S. Valley View
    Las Vegas, NV   89103
    (702) 368-1717

NEVADA GAMING SCHOOL
3100 Sirius Avenue
Las Vegas, NV   89102
(702) 873-2345

NEVADA SCHOOL OF DEALING
116 N. Third Street
Las Vegas, NV   89101
(702) 385-3325

OPERA HOUSE DEALERS SCHOOL
2121 Las Vegas Blvd. North
North Las Vegas, NV   89030
(702) 649-2929

PROFESSIONAL DEALERS SCHOOL OF AMERICA
770 Fremont
Las Vegas, NV   89101
(702) 382-1478

STRIP DEALERS SCHOOL
2309 Las Vegas Blvd. South
Las Vegas, NV   89104
(702) 731-1010

STRIP SLOT REPAIR SCHOOL
    1102 Fremont
    Las Vegas, NV   89101
    (702) 388-2855

VEGAS DEALING SCHOOL
    415 Carson Avenue
    Las Vegas, NV   89101
    (702) 477-7744

There are many other trade schools in Las Vegas which teach a vocation, in addition to the University of Nevada Las Vegas and the Community College of Southern Nevada. A listing of some of the vocations taught at local trade schools is as follows:

        Air Conditioning/Heating
        Bartending
        Broadcasting
        Business Courses
        Carpentry/Cabinet Making
        Cocktail Waitress
        Computer Skills
        Contractors
        Court Reporting
        Drafting

Electronics
Floral Design
Hair Design
Insurance
Interior Design
Medical Assistant
Pet Grooming
Real Estate
Restaurant Management
Secretarial
Stockbroker
Travel/Airline Training
Trucking

There is a complete listing of schools with addresses and phone numbers in the telephone book yellow pages. Fees vary, so check with the individual school to find the costs for training in the field that you are interested in.

♥ ♣ ♦ ♠ ♥ ♣ ♦ ♠

THE LAS VEGAS CONVENTION AND VISITORS AUTHORITY

The Las Vegas Convention and Visitors Authority (LVCVA) markets Southern Nevada as a tourist destination and convention site. The Authority is funded by an 8% room tax and has a budget of $52 million dollars. Half of that budget is spent on marketing.

The Executive Director of the LVCVA is Manny Cortez, a well-liked and highly respected former County Commissioner. The LVCVA employs approximately 325 people, and has additional offices in London, Tokyo, Germany, and Brazil. The Director of Marketing is Rossi Ralenkotter, whose job it is to insure that Las Vegas is marketed all over the world. He and his "ever-traveling" crew must be doing something right because in 1990 alone, Las Vegas enjoyed a grand total of 2,241,000 foreign visitors who spent over $1,107,100,000. These figures do not include the visitors from the United States nor the dollars they spent, nor do these figures reflect what was waged at the gaming tables.

The Convention Center is now able to offer over 1,700,000 sq. ft. of convention space. It is located at 3150 Paradise Road, right next to the Las Vegas Hilton. The phone number is (702) 733-2323. In addition to the convention facilities at the Main Convention Center, most of the major hotels have vast amounts of convention space, which assists in allowing even the largest of conventions to hold their affair in our fair city. There are very few cities that can offer as much diversity in sites and entertainment or as much convention and hotel space as Las Vegas.

When a very large convention arrives in Las Vegas, such as the COMDEX convention, there is a vast number of temporary jobs to be had in all areas connected with putting on a convention of this size. Registration desk jobs, models, tour guides, runners, photographers, food service personnel, and taxi and limousine drivers are just a few of the areas where extra help is usually needed. Since there are several very large conventions yearly, people in the temporary employment field can be kept fairly busy.

One such "temporary employee" I spoke with often serves as a tour guide for various convention coordinating companies. Marie Pelliccioni is kept extremely busy because she has a knack for turning an ordinary tour into a most enjoyable experience for the tourists. She also has lived in this city for twenty years and loves it as much as I do! Her part-time work schedule turns into more hours than a full-time employee during the busy convention season from September through April. She loves her "part-time" work because on one day she may be hosting a bus load of tourists to Mt. Charleston, the next day she may be taking a large group to a show at one of the big hotels, and the next day she may be commentating a fashion show or greeting a plane load of tourists at the airport. Whatever it is she's doing, she's enjoying it because she's meeting people from all over the world. She is definitely a "people person". She is representative of the friendly and courteous type of people who call Las Vegas "home".

♥ ♣ ♦ ♠ ♥ ♣ ♦ ♠

Some interesting statistics and information have been passed on to us by the State of Nevada Employment Security Division:

- Nevada and Arizona are expected to show the fastest growth rate in total income, jobs and population between 1991 and the year 2000.

- The population of Clark County is fast approaching 900,000 people.

- Visitor numbers continue to swell and are now approaching 22 million annually.

- The school district recruited 1000 new teachers in 1990, 800 in 1991, and many more since then. They now have 182 schools, over thirty of which have been built in the last three years.

OPENING A BUSINESS IN CLARK COUNTY

If you are going to start a new business in Las Vegas, it would be wise to consult a business attorney to assist you in filing corporation or partnership papers with the State of Nevada. If your new business is a sole proprietorship, the process is simpler, but a discussion with a good attorney is wise anyway. A sole proprietorship allows someone to sue you, personally, if something goes wrong involving your business. If you have questions about forming a corporation, you may call the Nevada Secretary of State's Office in Carson City at (702) 885-5105.

Before leasing or purchasing a building to house your business, you must call the Planning Department in the Public Service Building to learn if the type of business you wish to operate at the address is allowed by the Zoning Department. Their number is (702) 455-4314. When leasing a building, you will probably be required to post first and last month's rent.

You must file a Fictitious Firm Name (the name you will be doing business under) with the County Clerk's office. This can be done by going to the bank you will be doing business with to obtain the proper paperwork. You must have the paperwork notarized and then take it to the County Clerk's office in the Clark County Courthouse located at 200 South Third Street, Third Floor. This is in downtown Las Vegas. The cost to file these papers is $15 in cash, and you must have this paperwork in hand when you go to the licensing department to file for your business license. Some of the local banks will file the papers for you, thus saving you a trip to the County Clerk's office. However, they usually charge $10 - $15 extra for that service.

If your new business will be selling merchandise, you must apply for a Resale Number with the Nevada Department of Taxation, 2501 East Sahara Avenue (486-4050). A deposit is required which is equal to 21% of your estimated gross sales for the first month. Once in business, the sales tax you will collect from your customers is 7%. You will need a copy of this Resale Certificate when you apply for your business license.

For a corporation, you must have incorporation papers, approved by the Secretary of State, as well as a listing of current officers, before applying for a business license.

If you are sharing an office with another business, you will need a letter of authorization from that business. If you are leasing or purchasing a building, you will need either a copy of the lease agreement or sales contract.

A health permit will be required before applying for a business license if you will be selling food products in your business. Call the Health Department at (702) 383-1258 for an inspection of your business location.

Most landlords require business insurance on your business, listing them as co-insured by you. You should get a competent insurance agent as soon as possible. Rates for business insurance vary greatly, so shop around. You will, of course, have to give the insurance company a deposit. Usually, this equals approximately three month's premium.

Utility deposits for your business will also vary depending on the type of business, number of hours operated per day, the size of the building, and your personal credit rating, unless your business has a previous track record. You can count on a "minimum" of a few hundred dollars deposit for each utility. The minimum deposit for Nevada Power is reportedly higher. In interviewing various business owners, the smallest deposit we were told about was $500 paid by a small (3000 sq. ft.) retail store. Larger businesses which we interviewed reported deposits as high as $2500 and more. Most of these deposits are returned within a year if you maintain an excellent payment record.

♥ ♣ ♦ ♠ ♥ ♣ ♦ ♠

BUSINESS LICENSING

Now that you have all the paperwork you need to file for a business license, you must decide whether your new business is in the city or county. Although the entire region is known as Las Vegas, there are many unincorporated areas which fall under Clark County, rather than the City of Las Vegas. You can determine which classification your business falls under by just calling either Clark County (455-4252) or the City of Las Vegas (386-6281).

CLARK COUNTY
BUSINESS LICENSE DEPARTMENT

333 South Sixth Street
Las Vegas, NV   89101
(702) 455-4252
8:00 AM - 4:30 PM, Monday - Friday

Here is a checklist of the necessary paperwork or information which you must present at the licensing department:

- Zoning approval
- Certificate of Incorporation
- Certificate of Fictitious Firm Name
- Letter of authorization if sharing an office with another business, or your lease or purchase agreement
- Sales Tax Certificate
- Health Permit (if applicable)

The initial licensing fee varies according to the type of business. The minimum fee is $100. There is also a $35 filing fee for filing all the paperwork.

If you are engaged in a business that requires a state license, you must obtain that before applying for your Clark County Business License. The businesses which require a state license are: real estate sales, insurance sales, contractors, beauty and barber shops, and used car sales. Additional information can be obtained on the state license you require by calling the respective business division of that profession listed in the telephone book white pages under "Nevada, State Of".

CITY OF LAS VEGAS
BUSINESS LICENSE DIVISION

400 East Stewart
Las Vegas, NV   89101
(702) 386-6281
8:30 AM - 4:30 PM, Monday - Friday

Some of the paperwork that is required to apply for a Clark County Business License is also necessary for applying for a license in the City of Las Vegas: Resale Certificate from the Department of Taxation, and a Health Permit from the Health Department (if you are handling food products). Corporation papers are not required if you are a corporation.

The fees to open a business in the city range from $50 semi-annually, depending on your gross revenues. There is no filing fee with the city.

* * * * * * *

Upon acquiring your business license, if you will have any employees, you will need to pay a visit to the offices of the Nevada State Industrial Insurance System (S.I.I.S.). Your employees must be covered by you for Workman's Compensation. You will be required to give a deposit to S.I.I.S. according to the type of business you have and the number of employees you will have. Upon opening the business, you will file your S.I.I.S. reports and make your payments monthly. The offices of the State Industrial Insurance System are located at 1700 W. Charleston (at the corner of Shadow Lane and West Charleston).

****

If you wish to buy an existing business in Las Vegas, there are several real estate companies which handle the sale of commercial properties. One such business is Swift Business Opportunities. They specialize in the sale of businesses with or without forcing you to purchase the building or land on which it is located. Linda Swift, owner of Swift Business Opportunities, informs us that 1993 was a booming year for the purchase of businesses in our area. In early 1994, after the California earthquake and the freezing cold and snow in the Midwest and East, Swift's offices were inundated with phone calls from business people from all over the country who had "had enough"! Her people worked 12 - 15 hour days trying to accommodate the influx of potential buyers.

♥ ♣ ♦ ♠ ♥ ♣ ♦ ♠

LAS VEGAS CHAMBER OF COMMERCE
and
NEVADA DEVELOPMENT AUTHORITY

The Las Vegas Chamber of Commerce has many booklets which can assist you in learning about Las Vegas. The Chamber is supported by the Las Vegas business community, and is located at 711 E. Desert Inn Road, near the Convention Center. Their phone number is (702) 735-1616. Membership dues are $235 per year. If you are establishing a business in Las Vegas, one of your top priorities should be to join the Chamber of Commerce as they assist in so many ways to promote your business. It is also a great way to meet other business people and establish friendships at their monthly get-togethers. The Chamber is a most beneficial organization with a lot of very nice people.

If you are interested in information on opening a new business or factory in the Las Vegas area, the Nevada Development Authority could probably be most helpful to you. They are located at 3900 S. Paradise Road. Their phone number is (702) 791-0000. The Nevada Development Authority assists new and expanding companies in all phases of facility site location and development, and they research answers for the questions a new business may have. This non-profit organization has greatly contributed to the continuing economic growth of our community. They have an excellent staff of top professionals who can guide you every step of the way in establishing your new business. The Nevada Development Authority has all the facts and figures at their fingertips to suggest what types of businesses could be highly successful in the Las Vegas area.

♥ ♣ ♦ ♠ ♥ ♣ ♦ ♠

BUSINESS ADVERTISING BUDGET

Too often, when people are setting up a new business, they forget to allow money for advertising. "Word of mouth" is great, but you have to get those first customers in there who can spread the word for you.

The two daily newspapers, the *Las Vegas Review Journal* and the *Sun*, are printed, sold, and distributed by the *Review Journal*, a Donrey Media Group newspaper. The *Review Journal* is a morning paper, and the *Sun* has an afternoon distribution. On Saturdays and Sundays, the two combine into one paper. The 1994 display advertising rates for both papers are indicated below. Going on a contract can give you lesser rates and an "in" to a lot of special discounts that the two newspapers offer.

NON-CONTRACT OPEN RATES
(Per column inch)

Daily Combo, Saturday or Holidays	Review Journal	Sun	Sunday
$66.33	$53.38	$38.37	$73.70

MONTHLY EARNED CONTRACT RATES

There is a minimum contract requirement of ten column inches each and every calendar month for six consecutive months. All rates are per column inch.

Column Inch Per Month	Daily Combo, Saturday or Holidays	Review Journal	Sun	Sunday
10"	58.67	43.32	31.87	60.30
18"	50.88	37.21	29.37	52.06
30"	50.11	36.87	28.50	51.53
55"	48.29	36.17	26.24	50.51
100"	47.71	35.90	25.62	49.99
150"	47.03	35.34	25.44	49.48
225"	46.47	34.92	25.01	48.63
375"	45.66	34.29	24.40	47.92
500"	44.72	33.60	24.09	46.89
750"	43.82	32.84	23.79	45.86
1500"	42.38	31.73	22.99	44.32
3000"	41.89	30.55	22.07	42.26
4500"	39.38	29.65	21.63	41.49
6000"	37.86	28.54	19.62	39.94

There are also several smaller weekly newspapers which cost from $5 per column inch to $15 per inch depending on the size of your ad.

Radio advertising rates depend on the time you wish to advertise, the show, and the frequency of the ad. Costs range from $25 for a 30-second ad to $100 for a 60-second spot.

The main local network television stations are Channel 3 (NBC), Channel 5 (Fox Network), Channel 8 (CBS) and Channel 13 (ABC). Again, the rates vary according to the time slots you choose and the frequency of your ad. Running late night, between midnight and 6:00 AM, could cost as little as $30 for a 30-second ad on some of the television stations, while "Prime Time" could cost as much as $600 for a 30-second ad.

Cable television offers some very good package rates, which are usually less than the major networks, so you may want to check them out.

If you are not an expert at writing your own commercials, you may wish to contact a reputable advertising agency. They usually have rates for all the media at their fingertips and can suggest to you where your advertising dollars would be most effective. They will also write your ad for you. Their commissions are usually paid to them from the media and not by you. They are often able to obtain better rates for you, too, because they place a vast amount of advertising for many clients.

Even on a limited budget, it is not unrealistic to give yourself a minimum of $6000 a month, for a few months, to get your advertising campaign off the ground.

Some people I know have hired a pubic relations firm rather than an actual advertising agency. The public relations firm gets favorable stories published about the business or the proprietor. These stories often create more traffic for the business than what an actual display ad or television commercial would.

Cindy Ingram and Associates, a public relations firm, advised us that the cost of this service could run from $100 - $150 each time a story about your business is published. That turns out to be considerably less expensive than a one-time shot in a daily newspaper display ad.

♥ ♣ ♦ ♠ ♥ ♣ ♦ ♠

CLARK COUNTY SCHOOL DISTRICT

Once you have an address in Las Vegas, you must call the Clark County School District at 799-5011 to locate the school that your child will attend. There are presently 164 elementary and secondary schools in the Las Vegas area, with more being added each year. We have the 14th largest school district in the nation with 128,000 students. The class size is about 25 students per teacher. In the Kindergarten through Second Grade levels, the pupil to teacher ratio in most schools is 16-1. A.C.T. and S.A.T. scores are above the national average.

Students coming from out of state must bring their grade transcripts from their previous school, and they must have proof of immunization. The immunization record is the same as is required in every other school district across the country. It must show shots for diphtheria, pertussis, tetanus, measles, and polio. The Clark County Health District at 625 Shadow Lane will offer these immunizations, free of charge, with proof of your child's age.

Our public school system offers special services and programs for the handicapped and retarded, bilingual programs for the academically talented, and vocational training for those students wishing to train for a trade in which they can be employed directly after high school. Horizon High School was implemented for high school students who have to work for a living or are young parents. This school has flexible hours to work around the students' schedules. The Parks and Recreation Department offers many athletic programs for students in addition to what is offered by the school district.

Students graduating from high school in Clark County must have 23 credits, as well as a computer class having been completed during their school years.

There are numerous parochial and private schools throughout the area, plus many preschools. A total listing under "Schools - Academic" can be found in the Las Vegas telephone book yellow pages.

Upon enrolling your student in school, become involved with the Parent - Teacher Association. Be involved with your child's education, and be aware of the progress he is making. Although we have excellent teachers, they can't do it alone!

♥ ♣ ♦ ♠ ♥ ♣ ♦ ♠

A WAY TO A HIGHER EDUCATION

Two years ago, a Las Vegas restaurant owner's minor problem turned out to be a "solution" for one of his hard-working waitresses. It seems she had a fifteen-year-old son and a sixteen-year-old nephew who had decided, at that time, that they were not going to go on to college upon graduation. They decided they would each get a job when they turned eighteen. They wouldn't waste four more years of their life sitting in school. Their reasoning was that they would have a four-year jump on earnings if they skipped college.

The "solution" came on one of Las Vegas' very hot summer nights. The restaurant's commercial dishwasher broke down. That meant the dishes had to be washed by hand. The two dishwashing fellows who worked there said, "No way!" and walked off the job, leaving the kitchen in turmoil. It was a very busy Friday night and the lack of clean dishes would have resulted in turning away at least an additional 150 people who had reservations.

The waitress called her son and nephew and asked how they would each like to make $5.00 an hour for the next seven hours. The idea of making some unexpected money appealed to them, so they jumped in the car and went to the restaurant. Afterwards, to hear these two boys tell it, it was the story of "Seven Hours in Hell". The waitress had failed to tell them that the room they would be working in was not cooled with an air conditioner, but by a swamp cooler which gives off moist air. Using very hot water to wash dishes, coupled with a scalding hot sprayer to rinse them, in a tiny room where moisture surrounds you, resulted in 100% humidity. In addition to this, the actual temperature in that room didn't get below 85 degrees since the temperature outside was 115.

When the boys arrived, there were already stacks and stacks of dirty dishes waiting for them, and as the evening wore on, the stacks grew higher. The waitresses continued bringing in more. Toward the end of the evening, the boys thought they saw the light at the end of the tunnel. The stacks began dwindling. Then suddenly, the chef's helper appeared with enough dirty pots and pans to fill a room in itself. Over 300 dinners had been served that night.

The two boys thought they would faint! The nephew said, "I'm going to be sure to never miss church on Sunday anymore! I'm sure this is what Hell is like and I want no part of it!" His aunt, the waitress, said "No. This is what it's like if you don't get a college education. These are about the only kinds of jobs that would be available to you."

Both boys went on to college after high school, and we are delighted to report that both obtained excellent jobs upon graduation. Neither wish to ever see the inside of a restaurant kitchen again, so it is a safe bet that they won't consider becoming restauranteurs.

****

Some people change their ways when they see the light...Others only when they feel the heat.

UNIVERSITY OF NEVADA, LAS VEGAS
4505 South Maryland Parkway
Las Vegas, NV   89154
(702) 739-3011

The University of Nevada, Las Vegas (UNLV) is listed in *U.S. News & World Report* as one of the top up and coming universities in the United States. There are approximately 19,000 students enrolled. The tuition for Las Vegas residents is $58 per credit. This is extremely reasonable as compared to most universities across the country. If a student is carying a full load per semester (12 credits), it would cost $696, or $1,392 per year, plus books. The books for the year could run between $300 - $400. The major programs of specialization offered are:

> College of Arts and Letters
> College of Business & Economics
> College of Education
> College of Engineering
> College of Health Sciences
> College of Hotel Administration
> College of Science & Mathematics

All UNLV programs are accredited by the Northwest Association of Schools &

Colleges. The College of Hotel Administration is known to be one of the finest in the nation. In addition to the great educational opportunities and sports programs at UNLV, there are many cultural groups that have been formed in music, drama, dance, and art. There are cultural events to attend weekly for both university students and the general public.

The Las Vegas community and gaming industry have backed the University tremendously since its inception in 1957. Much expansion has been done, and efforts to recruit some of the top professors and teachers in the country have proven very successful. Everyone in the United States probably saw the "Rebels" demonstrate their phenomenal basketball skills in 1990-91, but basketball is not the only sport at UNLV. There are fourteen intercollegiate teams, and most can be described as up and coming.

♥ ♣ ♦ ♠ ♥ ♣ ♦ ♠

COMMUNITY COLLEGE OF SOUTHERN NEVADA
3200 E. Cheyenne
North Las Vegas, NV   89030
(702) 643-6060

Enrollment at the Community College of Southern Nevada currently exceeds 27,000 students. Students earn degrees in Applied Science, Associate of Arts, and Associate of General Studies. Many students later transfer their credits to four-year colleges. Certificates of Achievement can be earned in courses specially designed to improve various job skills. In addition to the main campus listed above, the College also has two branch campuses listed below. Course catalogs listing the wide variety of programs available can be obtained by contacting any of the three campuses. The West Charleston facility is a training center mainly for medical positions.

HENDERSON CAMPUS
700 College Drive
Henderson, NV   89014
(702) 564-7484

CLAUDE I. HOWARD
HEALTH SCIENCES CENTER
5375 W. Charleston Blvd.
Las Vegas, NV   89102
(702) 877-1133

There are many programs offered for adult education throughout the city. Information can be obtained by calling UNLV, the Community College of Southern Nevada, or Adult Education Services.

♥ ♣ ♦ ♠ ♥ ♣ ♦ ♠

SENIORS

Fourteen percent of Nevada's population is comprised of seniors. They retire to Las Vegas for most of the same reasons that younger people come here: affordable housing, low taxes, and good climate. After interviewing many seniors, we found that most of them have worked hard throughout their lives and now want to relax and enjoy themselves.

Where better to do it but the city of 24-hour entertainment? Not only are there golf courses and outdoor recreational activities which can be enjoyed year round, but there is also gambling. Bingo, with its big money prizes, is especially popular. Most bingo rooms at the casinos open early in the morning and run games every other hour until 1:00 - 2:00 AM.

Some of the hotels have specials for seniors which include discounted or "two for one" meals, free bingo, special senior gaming tournaments and/or free gifts. Some also have their own casino vans which travel to the adult mobile home parks and adult housing communities to give seniors a free ride to their casinos. The hotels also offer lounge and main showroom entertainment that is second to none. Several of the hotels begin their lounge entertainment in the afternoon, and have continuous shows until 3:00 - 4:00 AM.

The Howard W. Cannon Senior Citizens Center located at 340 N. Eleventh Street is the site for all State services for seniors, and also houses the offices of AARP. Once a month, the Nevada Department of Motor Vehicles comes to the Cannon Center to renew driver's licenses for senior citizens. The Center has a lot of information and services to offer seniors, including a "Sunshine Bus" which takes the homebound senior or a non-driver to the doctor, other appointments or on errands. The cost for this is $1.00 - $2.00.

Seniors can also take advantage of "Meals on Wheels", "Brown Bag Lunches", and special trips. The senior population continues to grow rapidly because of the great climate and overall benefits of living in our beautiful desert.

For seniors age 62 or older, no deposits on utilities are required at Nevada Power Company, Southwest Gas, and the Las Vegas Water District. Centel may ask for a deposit if you did not have previous phone service or if you have bad credit. To find out if you qualify for no deposit with Centel, call 1-800-877-7077.

Thinking of getting wiser in your old age? Both the University of Nevada and the Community College of Southern Nevada want to help you do that. They offer free classes to youngsters over age 62 who wish to get a higher education. The free classes are based on space availability. It's a terrific opportunity to delve into areas of study that you didn't have the time, or perhaps the money, to do when you were younger. So get out your sneakers and bobby socks and walk yourself to the nearest place of higher education to pick up some new ideas, or perhaps a new life.

Las Vegas is a terrific place to spend your senior years. A lot of people claim that it has done wonders for their asthma or arthritis. Isn't it time for you to be entertained and enjoy life a bit? Come to Las Vegas!

♥ ♣ ♦ ♠ ♥ ♣ ♦ ♠

SENIOR HEALTH CARE

A new service for seniors is offered to Nevada residents by doctors. It's called Nevadacare, and is available to anyone with Medicare (Part B), and earning less than $32,000 a year (couple) or $25,000 a year (single). With Nevadacare, participating doctors agree to charge you no more than what Medicare allows per visit. This does not apply to hospital costs or laboratory fees, only the doctor's fee. The card is free, and an application is available by writing to:

**NEVADA STATE
MEDICAL ASSOCIATION**
3660 Baker Lane, #101
Reno, NV 89509
1-800-828-0164

Nevadacare is not an insurance policy. It is only an assurance by participating doctors that you will pay no more than Medicare allows.

Many hospitals have special plans they offer free of charge, or for a very small fee, to seniors who wish to register with them. There is a wide range of savings and special programs offered. Check with the various hospitals to see exactly what is offered, and what would be the most advantageous for you. Some hospitals accept Medicare and your supplemental insurance as payment in full if you are registered with them.

♥ ♣ ♦ ♠ ♥ ♣ ♦ ♠

HOW FAR CAN YOU STRETCH YOUR SOCIAL SECURITY?

For the past nine years, a retired couple from Wisconsin have been coming to Las Vegas for the winter. They normally arrive around October 1st and depart around April 1st. Since they keep track of their expenses and what they spend on recreation, they were the perfect couple from whom to get an idea of the cost of living for "snowbirds". We'll call them Joe and Betty.

First of all, driving to Las Vegas from their home in Wisconsin takes approximately two and a half days. The distance is 2000 miles, and Joe says it takes about 100 gallons of gas for his car. Gasoline prices fluctuate from year to year, and from state to state. This year, the cost averaged out to $1.25 a gallon, or $125. Joe said he thought the price for the return trip would be approximately the same.

When on the road, Joe and Betty stay in motels which cost between $30 and $40 per night. Joe says there is a good selection in that price range. The on-the-road meal costs average about $25 a day for the couple. They are both light eaters, so someone with a voracious appetite might spend more.

When Joe and Betty arrive in Las Vegas, they immediately begin their quest for a furnished apartment. They often call ahead, from their home in Wisconsin, and have one waiting for them. When they do that, they are assured of a place to live. They then call Nevada Power Company and have the electricity turned on as of the day they plan to arrive. Sometimes due to the massive influx of snowbirds to Las Vegas, they are unable to acquire a furnished apartment in one of their favorite complexes just by calling. Therefore, upon their arrival, they start checking the various furnished apartments around town, usually in the general vicinity of the Strip (Las Vegas Blvd. South).

Over the years, Joe and Betty have been able to rent a nice one bedroom or studio for under $400 a month. The average price ranges from $350 - $525. However, some of the newer, larger apartments can cost as high as $750 - $900. It all depends on your tastes and budget. This past winter, Joe and Betty paid $375 a month, plus their electricity, which averaged about $40 a month. In addition, their monthly phone service was $12.25 plus the cost of any long distance calls they made.

Since they are early risers, Joe and Betty take advantage of all the terrific 99¢ breakfast specials at the various hotel/casinos. These specials usually end at 7:00 AM, but as long as your order is placed by 7:00 AM, you get it for 99¢. When breakfast is that inexpensive, it's kind to leave at least a $1.00 tip (for two people). Therefore, a breakfast for two can cost only $3.10 - $3.25, including tax and tip. That works out to $97.50 per month to have breakfast out daily. Their grocery bill adds up to about $30 a week ($120 per month). About once a week, Joe and Betty take advantage of one of the nice buffets for lunch or dinner. That adds about $8.00 more to their weekly budget.

While in Las Vegas this past year, Joe and Betty put a total of 3800 miles on their car which cost them approximately $52 a month in gasoline. That included various sightseeing excursions outside of the city.

This is a total monthly breakdown of the 1993/94 living expenses in Las Vegas for Joe and Betty:

Rent	$375.00
Electricity	40.00
Phone	13.00
Breakfasts	97.50
Groceries	120.00
Gasoline	52.00
Buffets	32.00
TOTAL	**$729.50**

That's for two people. Their two social security checks more than cover these basic living expenses. They had entertainment charges on top of that, but since Joe has been able to acquire a part-time job in Las Vegas every year, he allows the money that he earns to be used for that.

Although Joe's part-time jobs have only paid $6.00 an hour, he manages to earn between $150 - $175 a week. He enjoys his part-time work. It gives him something extra to do, as well as giving him and his wife their weekly entertainment fund. His winter jobs over the past few years have included salesman at a furniture liquidation center, a part-time desk clerk at a motel, a cashier at a 7-11 store, a runner for the housekeeping department of a major motel, and a "Mr. Fix-It" for a gentleman who owned rental properties. Joe did such a good job for the people who owned the furniture liquidation center that they have held a position open for him for the past four winters. Joe is 73 years old, and believes in the good old American work ethic. On top of that, he's very helpful, kind, and friendly. So it only goes to show that if you really want to work and you are a good employee, there are jobs out there for you, regardless of your age.

There are many people here who are unemployed because, where they come from, they were making $10 - $20 an hour, and they wouldn't think of working for anything less than that! Those people, with that type of attitude, usually stay unemployed a long time!

Snowbirds and permanent residents alike find they get more out-of-town guests than they ever did living anywhere else. Joe and Betty have visitors from out-of-state more than once a month during their stays in Las Vegas. Yes, Las Vegas is the land of opportunity, sunshine, and fun. It is also the land of unexpected visits from many friends and relatives, some that you hardly knew you had!

Snowbird's paradise? "Yes," say Joe and Betty. "We wouldn't have come here nine years in a row if it wasn't!"

A note to add to this story: Joe and Betty, who have Medicare and a supplemental insurance, went to a nearby Las Vegas hospital and joined, what they called, the Seniors' Hospital Club. If either one of them becomes ill while here, they can go to that hospital and be assured that whatever Medicare and the supplemental insurance pays is all they will be charged. Even residents who are only in Las Vegas a few months out of the year can register at no charge at any of several area hospitals.

♥ ♣ ♦ ♠ ♥ ♣ ♦ ♠

GETTING MARRIED IN LAS VEGAS

Las Vegas is very popular for couples getting married, and the main reason is that a blood test is not required, and there is no waiting period. You can go to the Clark County Marriage License Bureau, get your license, and get married ten minutes later. Valentine's Day seems to be the most popular wedding day of the year. Every wedding chapel in the city is booked on that day, and reservations are definitely required.

The cost of the marriage license is $35 (cash only), which can be acquired at the Marriage License Bureau located at 200 S. Third Street in Downtown Las Vegas. Their hours of operation are from 8:00 AM - Midnight, Monday through Thursday. On weekends they open at 8:00 AM on Friday and stay open until Midnight on Sunday night. On legal holidays they also stay open 24 hours. Their phone number is (702) 455-4415.

Other costs involved in a Las Vegas wedding include the cost of the actual ceremony (around $50), the cost of renting the chapel (around $50, but varies depending on the chapel you use), and then there are the extras you may or may not want, such as flowers, music, pictures, etc. A rough estimate of how cheaply you can get married in Las Vegas would probably be around $135 - $160 (including the cost of the license). That is definitely a "no-frills" wedding.

We counted 38 wedding chapels in the yellow pages, and they all offer "packages", some of which include flowers, music, pictures, videos, limousines, etc. You can make all your arrangements when you arrive in Las Vegas. You can even rent a tuxedo or a spectacular wedding gown if you wish. Designer Rentals at 4559 W. Flamingo (364-GOWN) offers a selection of over 400 bridal gowns, dresses, and suits that can make your wedding day complete.

There is a chapel in Las Vegas now that has "drive-thru" service. Yes, you can now get married without leaving the comfort of your automobile. This service is available at the Little White Chapel, and others will probably be following suit shortly. It's an ideal situation for people with a fast-paced life who don't have a lot of time on their hands. One young fellow commented that since he spends so much time at fast food "drive-thru's", why not continue his lifestyle and have a "drive-thru" wedding?! Interesting concept.

Many of the hotels have wedding chapels located within their property and offer complete honeymoon packages too. Some of these include The MGM Grand, Treasure Island, Tropicana, Riviera, Harrah's, Bally's, Excalibur, and the Imperial Palace.

****

Since marriages are so popular in our city (over 75,000 couples married here last year), we are forced to touch on the subject of divorce. That also happens, unfortunately. To get a divorce in Nevada, you must be a resident for a minimum of six weeks. Once that obligation is fulfilled, you can then file for your divorce, and usually obtain it in two to three days if it is uncontested. It is wise to have a lawyer file all the necessary paperwork for you. Their fees could run anywhere from $500 and up. Nevada is a community property state. If you live here with your spouse and things start breaking up, plan to split everything 50-50.

An even better plan would be to try communicating with your spouse. You never know what you might work out.

♥ ♣ ♦ ♠ ♥ ♣ ♦ ♠

VALET THIS & VALET THAT

Recently, my sister-in-law from Chicago spent a month with us. During her stay, we did a few "touristy" things, but basically our day to day routine was our normal lifestyle. Some things though, which we considered "normal", totally amazed our guest. Some of the daily conveniences which we take for granted are not readily available in other cities. This was brought to my attention by Lenore (my sister-in-law).

When my husband took his clothes to the cleaners, Lenore laughed and said, "How lazy can you get?!" The cleaners had a "car hop" who came out to the car and issued a receipt for the clothing after she had taken it.

The following evening, Lenore and I went to the hospital to visit a sick friend. I pulled up at the front door and gave my car to the valet there. Lenore couldn't believe that the hospital had valet service. She said she'd had occasion to visit people in numerous Chicago-area hospitals, and to her knowledge, not one of the hospitals had valet parking. The cost for the valet parking was just a tip to the valet attendant. There was no charge for the actual parking space. This is the scenario for most all of our major hotels.

We are a bit spoiled in this respect, I guess. It came as quite a surprise to us when valet parking charges were added to our hotel bill on a recent trip to California. The valet charges were $7.50 a night to park our car, plus $2.50 each time we took the car out of the parking area. My husband questioned the front desk on what that extra $27.50 was on our bill, and when they said, "Valet parking," he couldn't believe it. I reasoned with him that since land prices are so much higher in California than in Las Vegas, they must be forced to charge for every square inch of space used. My sister-in-law informed me that the same holds true for many of the high-rise hotels in the Chicago area.

Although Lenore made fun of how lazy we were to valet park our cars all the time, she appreciated it very much when I did so at my favorite shopping mall. When we finished shopping, she was loaded down with gifts she had bought for everybody back home. Her feet were killing her, so it was really very nice for the car to be brought right to us rather than scouting out into the huge parking lot. It was well worth the $2.00 tip! My usual rule of thumb for tipping a valet is $1.00 if it takes them awhile to get my car, or $2.00 - $3.00 if they get it in a hurry!

I wouldn't exactly say we're "lazy" here in Las Vegas. It's just that we enjoy many of life's finer things, and that includes low cost valet parking!

****

Nothing adds as much interest and excitement to our lives as something that is clearly none of our business!

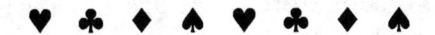

♥ ♣ ♦ ♠ ♥ ♣ ♦ ♠

SHOPPING

One of the things residents often mention is how much they like the fact that our major grocery stores are open 24 hours. It is not unusual to see a lady unloading groceries from her car at 2:00 AM. A lot of people say that after midnight is the best time to shop because the store is not crowded. There are also drive-thru dry cleaners that are open 24 hours, as well as some auto parts stores.

The major grocery chains here in Las Vegas include Albertsons, Lucky, Smith's Food King, and Vons. There are many other smaller grocery stores that are not part of a chain but who also have competitive pricing. We have many ethnic delicatessens, butcher shops, bakeries, and specialty food stores, just like any other metropolitan city.

Major department stores include Sears, J.C. Penney, Montgomery Wards, Woolworths, Broadway Southwest, Bullocks, May Company, K-Mart, Wal-Mart, Saks Fifth Avenue, Nieman Marcus, Dillards, Mervyns, and Target.

In the past few years, many major "discount" or "off-price" stores have opened here also. These include Marshalls, T.J.

Maxx, Ross Dress for Less, Payless Drugs, Quality Liquidators, Biz Mart, The Home Club, Costco, Service Merchandise, Anna's Linens, Strouds, Sam's Club, plus many more.

Las Vegas has three major shopping malls. The one that most newcomers see first is the Fashion Show Mall. It is right on the Las Vegas Strip, on the corner of Las Vegas Boulevard and Spring Mountain Road. It houses over 140 stores and restaurants. The Boulevard Mall on Maryland Parkway, between Desert Inn and Twain, houses over 80 stores and shops, and is adding more. The Meadows Mall, which is situated between Valley View and Decatur, right next to Highway 95 North, boasts over 145 stores, in addition to several fast food shops and restaurants. There are numerous smaller malls throughout the city, so wherever you live, you are usually within ten minutes of a full service shopping center.

If a new car is what you need, you may wish to start checking in the vicinity of Boulder Highway and East Sahara, and then travel west on Sahara to Eastern. You may also want to drive west on Sahara beyond Decatur, or try Tropicana, west of Interstate 15 South. There are a vast amount of car dealerships congregated in those areas. There are a few others on Rancho Road just south of Sahara, and many individual lots spread throughout the city.

Many of the rental car agencies liquidate their inventory of cars that are one to two years old. Usually some very good bargains can be had on used cars there, as well as at the regular car dealers.

****

A young gentleman from Pennsylvania who had relocated to Las Vegas was having extreme problems with his old beat-up car that had brought him to his new home. It was suggested that he buy a new one since he was now well-established in a job. He replied, "I follow my father's words of wisdom. He said, 'Some people put their money in the bank. Others park it in their driveways!' I prefer to put mine in the bank."

GROCERY SHOPPING

As previously mentioned, our major grocery stores are open 24 hours. To give you an idea of basic grocery prices, we checked one of the major chains that advertises that their prices are lower "over-all". Of course, all the stores advertise that they have lower prices, so upon arrival here, check them out! Below is a basic price list of what is charged at one major chain (as of March 15, 1994):

1 lb. loaf of store-brand bread	.49
1 gallon 2% nonfat milk (store brand)	2.27
10 lb. bag of russet potatoes	1.98
1 lb. sliced bacon	1.59
1 dozen large grade AA eggs	1.29
2 lb. lean ground beef	3.98
1 whole chicken	3.76
7 cans store-brand vegetables (45¢ ea)	3.15
1 lb. fresh perch	3.69
5 lb. red delicious apples	2.29
Roll store brand paper towels	.50
1 lb. margarine	.53
TOTAL	**25.52**

Many of the grocery stores are full service with a pharmacy, delicatessen, photo developing, snack bar, video rentals, and some even have a bank inside. There are more grocery stores being built throughout the city, so wherever you live, you are usually quite close to one.

♥ ♣ ♦ ♠ ♥ ♣ ♦ ♠

BEATING THE RECESSION

Over the many years when financial troubles loomed throughout the country, Las Vegas seemed to be immune. It was "business as usual" in most parts of the city. If our casinos were flourishing, it created a ripple effect, and most of the rest of the city flourished too. People still came to Las Vegas from all parts of the world and tried to win that extra money they needed to get by.

This past recession lasted much longer, and although Las Vegas still had lots of tourists, it seemed they were spending less money. Corporations which held their conventions in Las Vegas were beginning to scale down the number of people that they normally sent to the convention. There were also a number of other factors which forced the local population to tighten their purse strings as well. When this happened, many residents became financially creative. There were a few businesses that did quite well during the rough times because they were able to offer quality merchandise at a terrific savings. Their businesses were unique because they were selling "used".

Quality Liquidators at 4000 West Harmon is in the business of liquidating the furnishings of the major hotels when they renovate. The big hotels are not known for putting cheap furnishings in their properties, so Quality Liquidators offers solid wood bedroom sets, carpets, drapes, bedspreads, lamps, pictures, and living room furniture (from suites) at unheard of prices. They also liquidate furnishings of all kinds from businesses that are "going under", and from estates. You can usually find anything from pots and pans or office equipment, to exotic artwork and beautiful furniture. They advertise as a "Bargain Hunter's Paradise". Their warehouse, which is open to the public seven days a week, gets customers from all over the country. They have a steady flow of customers who stop in every other week just to browse and see what has come in that's different. Their inventory changes constantly and they get numerous "one-of-a-kind" items. They say that often they don't know what their trucks are bringing in until they arrive. The savings realized are anywhere from 40% - 80% off the cost of new, and some of the furniture looks like brand new!

Another place that has been equally successful in the liquidation business is the Irish Peddler at 501 North Main Street. They are located in an area where there are numerous other small, second-hand stores, but their variety and size, as well as the fact that they deal with the major hotels, makes them more or less the "King of the Road" in their neighborhood. Again, you can get quality at a good price in their establishment.

If baby clothes and baby furniture seem outrageously priced in the regular stores, a little establishment called Small Change at 3401 Sirius remedied that problem for many parents-to-be. They handle a vast array of "used, but not abused" baby clothes, furniture, and toys. Setting up a nursery can be a costly venture, but smart shoppers saved 30% - 50% when purchasing the used items. Some of the baby clothes looked like they had never been worn!

And if the ladies want designer clothes but can't see spending hundreds of dollars, there are many "resale shops" spread throughout the city. That's where the "moneyed" ladies bring their designer dresses and gowns to be resold to people who want quality, but who don't want to go broke getting it! I saw an exotic full length, beaded gown, identical to one I saw in a high-end department store for $1300. The resale shop's price was $400. The store was filled with beautiful dresses that ranged in price from $35 and up. These shops have been in business for many years so each has a good following of wealthy women who wish to dispose of their present wardrobes to make room for new.

There are many charitable organizations in Las Vegas that run thrift stores too. Their merchandise is all donated so they can sell items at greatly reduced prices also. These include Opportunity Village Association for Retarded Citizens at 921 South Main, St. Vincent Thrift Stores at 808 South Main (plus three other locations), Goodwill Industries at 3525 South Valley View, and five locations of the Salvation Army.

PUBLIC TRANSPORTATION

We must admit that the transportation system in Las Vegas falls short for anyone coming from a big city. But with our growth rate being what it is, the demand is being accommodated as quickly as possible, and many new routes have been established throughout the city. Two years ago, if you didn't live near the Strip (Las Vegas Boulevard), it was impossible to get to your casino job without a car. Now, if you live in outlying neighborhoods, there are buses to help you get to work. The buses are new, air-conditioned and the drivers are very helpful.

Monthly Pass	$20.00
Adult Cash Fare	$1.00
Senior Citizen Fare (65+)	.50
Senior Citizen Monthly Pass	$10.00
Handicap Fare	.50
Handicap Monthly Pass	$10.00

The Senior Citizen fare is available to persons 65 years of age and over who can show their Medicare card, driver's license, or identification card. Handicap fares are available for reason of illness, injury, age, congenital malfunction, or permanent or temporary incapacity or disability. A Medicare card must be shown at the time of fare purchase and when boarding the bus. Citizens Area Transit (CAT) operates handicap accessible buses on all routes, except when the vehicle is in for repair. The side entrance door is clearly marked with the symbol designating handicap accessible. Patrons requiring this service and wishing to verify that a particular route, at a specific time, has the handicap accessible bus may call 228-7433.

Children's Fare (Ages 5 - 17)	.50
Children Under 5	Free

Children under the age of five must be accompanied by a paying adult fare passenger. Transfer coupons must be requested and purchased from the driver at the time the fare is paid. Discount cards are available for purchase from the CAT Customer Service Center at the information booth at the Downtown Transportation Center, 300 North Casino Center Boulevard.

There are several taxicab companies in Las Vegas. The standard rates are $1.70 plus 20¢ per 1/7 mile. All are regulated by the

Taxicab Authority; therefore, all taxicab companies have the same rates.

If a limousine interests you, a standard limo costs $24.00 per charter hour, and a "stretch" limo costs $32.00 per charter hour.

Because our city has grown so rapidly, the streets and highway systems are expanding to improve all areas. At this time, you may find only one lane available on many streets because work is being done to widen roadways. Please bear with us now. Soon, all of our streets will be pleasurable to drive on.

♥ ♣ ♦ ♠ ♥ ♣ ♦ ♠

HOSPITALS

If you should be in need of any medical assistance, the following is a list of hospitals which serve the Las Vegas area:

COMMUNITY HOSPITAL
   1409 E. Lake Mead Blvd.
   North Las Vegas, NV 89030
   (702) 649-7711

DESERT SPRINGS HOSPITAL
   2075 E. Flamingo Road
   Las Vegas, NV 89119
   (702) 733-8800

HUMANA HOSPITAL SUNRISE
   3186 S. Maryland Parkway
   Las Vegas, NV 89109
   (702) 731-8000

UNIVERSITY MEDICAL CENTER
   1800 W. Charleston Blvd.
   Las Vegas, NV 89102
   (702) 383-2000

VALLEY HOSPITAL
   620 Shadow Lane
   Las Vegas, NV 89106
   (702) 388-4000

WOMENS HOSPITAL
   2025 E. Sahara Avenue
   Las Vegas, NV 89104
   (702) 735-7106

♥ ♣ ♦ ♠ ♥ ♣ ♦ ♠

CONVALESCENT HOSPITALS

SILVERCREST LAS VEGAS
   2170 E. Harmon
   Las Vegas, NV 89119
   (702) 794-0100

VEGAS VALLEY
CONVALESCENT HOSPITAL
   2945 Casa Vegas
   Las Vegas, NV 89109
   (702) 735-7179

REHABILITATION HOSPITALS

CAREUNIT HOSPITAL OF NEVADA
  5100 W. Sahara Avenue
  Las Vegas, NV 89102
  (702) 362-8404

CHARTER HOSPITAL
  7000 Spring Mountain Road
  Las Vegas, NV 89117
  (702) 876-4357

HCA MONTEVISTA HOSPITAL
  5900 W. Rochelle Avenue
  Las Vegas, NV 89103
  (702) 364-1111

♥ ♣ ♦ ♠ ♥ ♣ ♦ ♠

HOSPICES

NATHAN ADELSON HOSPICE
  4141 S. Swenson
  Las Vegas, NV 89119
  (702) 733-0320

Nellis Air Force Base also has their own hospital on the base. Many people have been working on the establishment of a veterans hospital in Las Vegas, and it appears that their efforts will soon pay off. We're keeping our fingers crossed.

****

A 74-year-old gentleman with a heart problem was advised that he would need a defibrillator implanted in order to survive. The cost of the unit, excluding doctor fees, was to be over $25,000. The man contemplated the doctor's words, then asked, "If this defibrillator fails and I die, can we get our money back?" The doctor smiled and replied, "Whichever way it goes, you'll end up with a bargain!"

P.S. The defibrillator worked wonders! He just celebrated his 75th birthday.

♥ ♣ ♦ ♠ ♥ ♣ ♦ ♠

FAVORITES

Each year, around the end of March, the *Review Journal/Sun* publishes a large list of what the local residents have voted as their favorite spots in Las Vegas for that year. Since this revised edition of *Getting Established in Las Vegas* is going to press before the end of March, we are unable to give you the 1994 list of favorites. However, as a longtime resident, I have a few favorites of my own that I can share with you.

In the restaurant category, I favor those with good food, good service, and reasonable prices. These include:

The Kitchen Cafe - 4850 W. Flamingo
North Beach Cafe - 2605 S. Decatur
Kiefer's (Top of the Carriage House -
    105 E. Harmon
Bob Taylor's Ranch House - 6250 Rio Vista
Pasta Palace (Palace Station Hotel) -
    2411 W. Sahara
Great Moments Room (Las Vegas Club
    Hotel) - 18 E. Fremont

There are several other restaurants which I find to have excellent food, but their prices may be a bit "spendy" for some. They are not on the list of places to dine several times a week, but if you wanted to treat yourself or a guest, you might try Morton's of Chicago Steakhouse in the Fashion Show Mall, or one of the two Ruth's Chris Steak Houses. Other good food can be found at Ferraro's Italian Restaurant on West Flamingo, Antonio's in the Rio Hotel, Caesar's Palace Bacchanal Room, Kokomo's at the Mirage, and several other gourmet establishments. We no longer "want" for good food in this town. We have a host of wonderful dining establishments for anyone's taste.

Although I am not a country western dancer myself, I am told that a favorite of the country western crowd is the Paladium on South Industrial, and Sam's Town on Boulder Highway. It seems everybody feels comfortable getting into the act and strutting their stuff at these places.

The Reggae Blues Club, downtown on Fremont and Fourth Street, is getting rave reviews from the college crowd, and older patrons as well. The people who are into swing dancing are patronizing the Gold Coast Hotel where they have the sounds of the Big Bands once a week.

The favorite "intimate" cocktail lounge voted best by the people of Las Vegas for a few years in a row was the Peppermill on the Strip across from the Stardust.

There are many sports bars around town, and each boasts that they have the most fun. Since I am not into the sports scene too much, I would have to let you find your own haunts in that department.

The locals' favorite casino hang-outs include the Palace Station, Gold Coast, Sante Fe, Rio, Sam's Town, and the Showboat. All of them offer super-duper meal deals and various promotionals to attract the locals. They do an excellent job of that, as is warranted by the crowds that are in their casinos constantly.

Bob Baskin Park, off Oakey and Rancho, is a great place to jog. Sunset Park at Eastern and Sunset is a nice place to have a picnic.

The best production show in the hotels is a toss-up between "Splash" at the Rivera, "Siegfried and Roy" at the Mirage, or "Cirque de Sole Mystere" at Treasure Island. Each is a very unique and spectacular production, and well worth seeing.

I am delighted to report that Las Vegas, after a time of bringing in fewer "big" names in entertainment, seems to be heading back to the big name agenda. We are also acquiring more Broadway shows. Yes, this definitely is the "Entertainment Capital of the World".

****

The simple things in life often present the best or most relaxing entertainment, such as reading a book, doing a crossword puzzle, writing a letter, putting together a jigsaw puzzle, trying your hand at a "paint-by-number", doing needlepoint or knitting, or taking up a hobby where you make something from scratch. Believe it or not, the residents of Las Vegas are really into those types of things as evidenced by our many successful hobby shops and bookstores.

♥ ♣ ♦ ♠ ♥ ♣ ♦ ♠

BREAKFAST SPECIALS

For those who stay up late (past midnight) or for those who rise very early, there are terrific savings to be had at various hotels for breakfast. Below is a listing of a few that we know about, but there are also many others throughout the city. This is what was being offered as of March 1994. Some of these may change somewhat during the year, but a good majority of them offer this type of breakfast special throughout the year.

ARIZONA CHARLIE'S
2 eggs, toast, bacon & hash browns - 49¢
Pancakes with bacon or sausage - 49¢
Midnight - 7:00 AM

BARBARY COAST HOTEL
Eggs & toast with ham or bacon or sausage - $1.95
11:00 PM - 7:00 AM

BOARDWALK CASINO
Bacon or sausage, eggs, toast & hash browns - $1.29
All the pancakes you can eat - 99¢
24 Hours

BOURBON STREET HOTEL
Ham or bacon or sausage, eggs, toast, & potatoes - 99¢
Pancakes - 99¢
Biscuits and Gravy - 99¢
10:00 PM - 6:00 AM

CONTINENTAL HOTEL
2 eggs, toast, hash browns, ham or bacon or sausage - 99¢
All you can eat pancakes - 75¢
11:00 PM - 11:00 AM

EL CORTEZ HOTEL
2 eggs, toast, potatoes, bacon, & coffee - 99¢
2 pancakes, bacon, & coffee - 99¢
Midnight - 5:00 AM

GOLD COAST HOTEL
Ham or sausage or bacon, eggs, toast, & potatoes - $1.99
Pancakes with ham or bacon - $1.99
Midnight - 6:00 AM

MAXIM HOTEL
2 eggs, toast, ham or bacon or sausage - 99¢
Midnight - 6:00 AM

PALACE STATION
2 eggs, toast, bacon or sausage, hash browns, & coffee - 99¢
11:00 PM - 6:00 AM

RIO SUITE HOTEL
T-bone steak 'n eggs - $2.99
11:00 PM - 11:00 AM

SANTA FE HOTEL
2 eggs, toast, bacon or sausage - 99¢
Midnight - 6:00 AM

SHOWBOAT HOTEL
Hotcakes & coffee - 89¢
French toast & coffee - 89¢
Biscuits and gravy - 89¢
11:00 PM - 7:00 AM

UNION PLAZA
2 eggs, toast, potatoes, bacon or sausage, & coffee - $1.99
24 Hours

♥ ♣ ♦ ♠ ♥ ♣ ♦ ♠

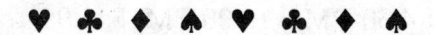

BUFFETS

Many of the hotels have breakfast, lunch and dinner buffets on a daily basis. Some are offered only on the weekends. The following is a partial listing of places you can go to get a vast abundance of some of the best food in the city, and at terrific prices.

ALADDIN
International Buffet
Breakfast, 7:30 AM - 10:30 AM, $3.95
Lunch, 11:00 AM - 3:00 PM, $4.95
Dinner, 4:00 PM - 10:00 PM, $5.95

ARIZONA CHARLIE'S
Wild West Buffet
Breakfast, 7:00 AM - 10:30 AM, $2.80
Lunch, 11:00 AM - 3:30 PM, $3.27
Dinner, 4:00 PM - 10:30 PM, $4.67

BALLY'S
Big Kitchen Buffet
Daily Brunch, 7:30 AM - 2:30 PM, $6.45
Dinner, 4:30 PM - 10:00 PM, $11.95

BOURBON STREET
Breakfast, 7:00 AM - 11:00 AM, $2.49
Lunch, 11:00 AM - 3:00 PM, $3.49
Dinner, 3:00 PM - 11:00 PM, $4.49

CAESARS PALACE
Palatium Buffet
Breakfast, Monday - Friday,
    7:30 AM - 11:00 AM, $6.50
Lunch, Monday - Friday,
    11:30 AM - 2:30 PM, $7.95
Saturday/Sunday/Holiday Brunch,
    7:30 AM - 2:30 PM, $11.95
Dinner, 4:30 PM - 10:00 PM, $11.95

CIRCUS CIRCUS
Breakfast, 6:00 AM - 11:30 AM, $2.29
Brunch, 12:00 PM - 4:00 PM, $2.99
Dinner, 4:30 PM - 11:00 PM, $3.99

CONTINENTAL
Florentine Room Buffet
Breakfast, $2.95
Lunch, $3.95
Dinner, $5.95

ELLIS ISLAND
Passport Buffet
Daily Lunch, 11:00 AM - 10:00 PM, $2.95

EXCALIBUR
RoundTable Buffet
Breakfast, 7:00 AM - 10:00 AM, $3.49
Lunch, 11:00 AM - 4:00 PM, $4.49
Dinner, 4:00 PM - 10:00 PM, $5.79

FITZGERALDS
Molly's Buffet
Breakfast, 7:00 AM - 11:00 AM, $3.99
Lunch, 11:30 AM - 4:00 PM, $4.49
Dinner, 5:00 PM - 9:00 PM, $5.99

FLAMINGO HILTON
Crown Room Buffet
Breakfast, 6:30 AM - Noon, $3.95
Dinner, 4:00 PM - 10:00 PM, $5.95
Children under 12, half price

FREMONT
Paradise Buffet
Breakfast, Monday - Friday,
    7:00 AM - 10:30 AM, $3.95
Lunch, Monday - Friday,
    11:30 AM - 3:00 PM, $4.95
Dinner, 4:00 PM - 10:00 PM
    (Saturday 4:00 PM - 11:00 PM), $7.95
Seafood Fantasy, Tuesday & Sunday,
    4:00 PM - 11:00 PM, $11.95

FRONTIER
Michelle's Village Cafe
Dinner, 4:00 PM - 10:00 PM, $5.95
Friday Seafood, $7.95
Beverage Extra

GOLD COAST
Breakfast, Monday - Saturday,
    7:00 AM - 10:30 AM, $2.45
Lunch, Monday - Saturday,
    11:00 AM - 3:00 PM, $3.45
Sunday Brunch, 8:00 AM - 3:00 PM, $4.45
Dinner, Nightly, 4:00 PM - 10:00 PM, $5.45
Includes frozen cocktail

GOLDEN NUGGET
The Buffet
Breakfast, Monday - Saturday,
   7:00 AM - 10:30 AM, $4.75
Lunch, Monday - Saturday,
   10:30 AM - 3:00 PM, $7.50
Dinner, 4:00 PM - 10:00 PM, $9.50
Children 4 - 10, half price excluding holidays

HACIENDA
El Grande Buffet
Breakfast, Monday - Saturday,
   7:00 AM - 11:00 AM, $3.95
Lunch, Monday - Saturday,
   11:30 AM - 3:00 PM, $4.95
Dinner, Nightly, 5:00 PM - 10:00 PM, $6.95

HARRAH'S CASINO
Breakfast, 7:00 AM - 11:00 AM, $3.79
Lunch, 11:00 AM - 5:00 PM, $3.99
Dinner 5:00 PM - 11:00 PM, $5.49

IMPERIAL PALACE
Emperor's Buffet
Breakfast, 7:00 AM - 11:00 AM, $3.99
Lunch, 11:00 AM - 4:30 PM, $4.49
Dinner, 5:00 PM - 11:00 PM, $4.99

LADY LUCK
Breakfast, 6:00 AM - 10:30 AM, $2.49
Brunch, 11:00 AM - 2:00 PM, $3.99
Dinner, 4:00 PM - 10:00 PM, $6.99

LAS VEGAS HILTON
Buffet of Champions
Breakfast, Monday - Friday,
    7:00 AM - 9:30 AM, $6.25
Lunch, Monday - Friday,
    11:00 AM - 2:30 PM, $7.99
Dinner, Nightly, 6:00 PM - 10:00 PM, $11.99
Children under 12 half price

LUXOR
Breakfast, 7:00 AM - 11:00 AM, $3.95
Lunch, 11:00 AM - 4:00 PM, $4.95
Dinner, 4:00 PM - 11:00 PM, $6.95
Children under 12 half price

MGM GRAND
Breakfast, 7:00 AM - 11:00 AM, $4.95
Lunch, 11:00 AM - 4:00 PM, $5.95
Dinner, 4:00 - 10:00 PM, $7.95

THE MAXIM
Evening Buffet, Daily,
    5:00 PM - 10:00 PM, $4.95

THE MIRAGE
Mirage Buffet
Breakfast, 8:00 AM - 10:45 AM, $6.50
Lunch, 11:00 AM - 2:45 PM, $8.50
Dinner, 3:00 PM - 9:30 PM, $10.25

PALACE STATION
Fisherman's Broiler
Seafood Soup 'n' Salad Bar,
    11:00 AM - 3:00 PM, $4.95
The Feast
Breakfast, Monday - Saturday,
    7:00 AM - 11:00 AM, $3.95
Lunch, Monday - Saturday,
    11:00 AM - 2:00 PM, $4.95
Dinner, Nightly, 4:30 PM - 10:00 PM, $7.95
Children under 12, $1.00 off

RIO SUITE
Carnival Buffet
Breakfast, 7:00 AM - 10:30 AM, $3.25
Lunch, 11:00 AM - 2:30 PM, $5.25
Dinner, 4:00 PM - 10:00 PM, $7.25
Brunch, Saturday & Sunday,
    7:00 AM - 3:00 PM, $6.25

RIVIERA
Breakfast, 7:00 AM - 10:00 AM, $4.95
Lunch, 11:00 AM - 3:00 PM, $4.95
Friday Seafood Fare,
    4:30 PM - 11:00 PM, $11.95

SAHARA
The Oasis
Breakfast, Monday - Saturday,
    7:00 AM - 11:00 AM, $4.95
Lunch, Monday - Saturday,
    11:30 AM - 2:30 PM, $5.95
Dinner, 4:00 PM - 10:30 PM, $6.95
Children under 7, half price

SAM'S TOWN
Uptown Buffet
Brunch, Monday - Friday,
    8:30 AM - 2:30 PM, $3.95
Dinner, Sunday - Thursday,
    4:00 PM - 9:00 PM, $6.49
    Friday - Saturday,
    4:00 PM - 10:00 PM, $6.49
Children under 6, half price

SANTA FE
Lone Mountain Buffet
Breakfast, 7:30 AM - 10:00 AM, $3.50
Lunch, 11:30 AM - 2:30 PM, $4.95
Dinner, 4:00 PM - 10:30 PM, $6.95

SHOWBOAT
Captain's Buffet
Lunch, Monday - Friday,
    10:00 AM - 3:30 PM, $4.45
    (Children under 12, $3.95)
Dinner, Monday - Thursday,
    4:30 PM - 10:00 PM, $6.45
    Saturday & Sunday,
    4:00 PM - 10:00 PM, $6.45
    (Children under 12, $4.95)
Lobster Buffet, Wednesday, $8.95
Brunch, Saturday & Sunday,
    8:00 AM - 3:00 PM, $5.45
    (Children under 12, $4.45)

STARDUST
Warehouse Buffet
Breakfast, Monday - Friday,
    7:00 AM - 11:00 AM, $4.95
Lunch, Monday - Friday,
    11:00 AM - 3:00 PM, $5.95
Dinner, Nightly, 4:00 PM - 10:00 PM, $7.95

TREASURE ISLAND
Breakfast, 7:00 AM - 10:45 AM, $4.99
Lunch, 11:00 AM - 3:45 PM, $6.99
Dinner, 4:00 PM - 10:00 PM, $8.99

VACATION VILLAGE
Breakfast, 6:00 AM - 11:00 AM, $3.95
Lunch, 11:00 AM - 5:00 PM, $4.95
Dinner, 5:00 PM - Midnight, $5.95

VEGAS WORLD
Moon Rock Buffet
Dinner, Daily, 4:30 PM - 10:00 PM, $4.95

WESTWARD HO CAFE
The Buffet
Breakfast, 7:00 AM - Noon, $4.95
Lunch, Noon - 4:00 PM, $4.95
Dinner, 4:00 PM - 10:00 PM, $5.95

♥ ♣ ♦ ♠ ♥ ♣ ♦ ♠

DINING GUIDE TO LAS VEGAS RESTAURANTS

($)	Inexpensive - Dinner under $10.00
($$)	Moderate - Under $20.00
($$$)	Expensive - Under $25.00
($$$$)	Very Expensive - $25.00 and over

* * * AMERICAN * * *

ALIAS SMITH & JONES
541 E. Twain, 732-7401 ($)
11:00 AM - 6:00 AM
Salads, sandwiches, fresh catch, beef stroganoff

BIG DOG'S BAR & GRILLE
1511 N. Nellis, 459-1099   ($)
6390 W. Sahara, 876-3647
24 Hours
Steaks, sausages, ribs, chicken, walleye

BOOGIE'S DINER OF ASPEN
Forum Shops at Caesars, 892-0860   ($)
11:00 AM - 11:00 PM
Friday & Saturday until 11:30 PM
Spicy wings, Reggie veggie melt, turkey burger

BOSTON GRILL & BAR
3417 S. Jones, 368-0750   ($)
24 Hours (Dinner 3:00 PM - 11:00 PM)
Beef stew in bread bowl, burgers, pastas

BRITTANY'S
7770 W. Ann Rd., 658-8998   ($$) Music
7:00 AM - 10:00 PM
Breakfast specials, burgers, salads, steak, shrimp

CAFE MICHELLE
1350 E. Flamingo, 735-8686 ($$) Music
11:00 AM - 11:00 PM
Patio dining, fresh fish, salads, crepes

CAFE NICOLLE
4760 W. Sahara, 870-7675 ($$) Music
11:00 AM - 11:00 PM (Sunday until 3:30 PM)
Patio dining, omelets, pastas, gourmet specialties

CAFFELATTE
4750 W. Sahara, 259-0686   ($)
8:00 AM - 4:00 PM, Closed Sunday
Sandwiches, salads, Belgian waffles, pastries

CALICO JACK'S
8200 W. Charleston, 255-6771   ($) Music
24 Hours
Steaks, BBQ ribs, honey-dipped fried chicken

CARLOS MURPHY'S
4770 S. Maryland Parkway, 798-5541 ($)
11:00 AM - 10:00 PM
   Friday/Saturday until 11:00 PM
Barbecue ribs, fajitas, mud pie

CASSIDY'S
Fitzgeralds Hotel, 388-2220 ($$)
Monday - Friday, 8:00 AM - 3:00 PM
Dinner, Nightly, 5:00 PM - 11:00 PM
Escargot, beef Wellington, orange roughy

CAVALIER
3850 E. Desert Inn, 451-6221 ($$) Music
Lunch, Monday - Friday, 11:00 AM - 3:30 PM
Dinner, Nightly, 5:00 PM - 11:00 PM
Steaks, seafood, prime rib, specialty dishes

CENTER STAGE
Union Plaza Hotel, 386-2512 ($$)
4:30 PM - 10:30 PM
Prime rib, chicken Sicilian, scampi maison

CHARCOAL ROOM
Hacienda Hotel, 739-8911 ($$)
5:00 PM - 10:30 PM
Friday & Saturday until 11:00 PM
Closed Monday & Tuesday
Special salads, black bean soup, T-bone steak

COACHMAN'S INN
3240 S. Eastern, 731-4202 ($$)
24 Hours
Prime rib, lamb chops, shrimp scampi, steaks

CORTEZ ROOM
Gold Coast Hotel, 367-7111 ($)
11:00 AM - 2:30 PM
Dinner, 5:00 PM - 11:00 PM
Mr. Terrible's porterhouse, swordfish

COUNTRY INN
2425 E. Desert Inn, 731-5035 ($$)
1401 S. Rainbow, 254-0520
7:00 AM - 10:00 PM
Friday and Saturday until 11:00 PM
Turkey, homemade biscuits, scones

COUSIN'S CAFE
1617 S. Decatur, 259-0282 ($)
3331 E. Tropicana, 451-5440
11:00 AM - 10:00 PM
Friday and Saturday until 11:00 PM
Chicken fried steak, Mama's meatloaf

ELLIS ISLAND
4178 Koval, 734-8638 ($$)
24 Hours
Steamed clams, seafood, steaks, barbecue fish

FERDINAND'S
5006 S. Maryland Pkwy, 798-6962   ($$)
9:00 AM - 11:00 PM
Steamers, prime rib, steaks, lobster

FLAMINGO ROOM
Flamingo Hilton Hotel, 733-3111 ($$)
Breakfast/Lunch, 7:00 AM - 2:00 PM
Dinner, 5:00 PM - 11:00 PM
Appetizer salad bar, seafood jambayala

T.G.I. FRIDAY'S
180 E. Flamingo, 732-9905 ($)
11:00 AM - Midnight
Sunday 10:00 AM - Midnight
Potato skins, firecracker shrimp, chicken

GARLIC CAFE
3650 S. Decatur, 221-0266   ($$) Music
4:30 PM - 10:30 PM
Ethnic antipasto counter, carpetbagger steak

GATES
2710 E. Desert Inn, 369-8010   ($) Music
11:00 AM - 10:00 PM
Thursday until Midnight,
Friday & Saturday until 2:00 AM
Sunday, Noon - 10:00 PM
Barbecue ribs, chicken, beef, ham

GOURMET CAFE
3560 Polaris, 362-9927   ($)
Monday - Friday, 8:00 AM - 3:00 PM
Soup, croissants, fresh baked banana bread

GREAT MOMENTS ROOM
Las Vegas Club, 385-1664   ($$)
5:30 PM - 10:30 PM
Flamed pepper steak, sauteed scalone

GREEN SHACK
2504 E. Fremont, 383-0007   ($$)   Music
5:00 PM - 9:30 PM, Closed Monday
Friday & Saturday 5:00 PM - 9:30 PM
Southern fried chicken, shrimp, orange roughy

GREENS SUPPER CLUB
2241 N. Green Valley Pkwy, 454-4211   ($$)
8:00 AM - 10:30 PM
Prime rib, steaks, veal, seafood, pasta

HARD ROCK CAFE
4475 Paradise, 733-8400   ($)
11:00 AM - 11:30 PM
Watermelon ribs, lime barbecue chicken

HILLTOP HOUSE
3500 N. Rancho, 645-9904   ($$)
5:00 PM - 10:00 PM, Closed Tuesday
Sunday/Monday, 5:00 PM - 9:00 PM
Steaks, chicken, seafood, pan-fried lobster tail

HOLY COW!
2423 Las Vegas Blvd. S., 732-2697   ($)
24 Hours
Rotisserie chicken and pork, ribs, bratwurst

JAVA CENTRALE
2295 N. Green Valley Pkwy, 434-3112   ($)
6:00 AM - 11:00 PM
Deli-style sandwiches, soups, specialty coffees

JEROME'S
4503 Paradise, 792-3772 ($$$) Music
Lunch, Monday - Saturday, 11:00 AM - 2:00 PM
Dinner, Nightly, 5:00 PM - 11:00 PM
Mussel saffron soup, pastas, Nob Hill veal

JITTERS GOURMET COFFEE
2457 E. Tropicana, 898-0056   ($)
6:00 AM - 11:00 PM
Sunday, 7:00 AM - 8:00 PM
Sandwiches, salads, quiche, scones

KATHY'S SOUTHERN COOKING
6407 Mt. Vista, 433-1005   ($)
11:00 AM - 9:45 PM/Sunday until 8:00 PM
Gumbo, chitlins, cornbread, pork ribs

KEUKEN DUTCH RESTAURANT
6180 W. Tropicana, 368-1077 ($)
24 Hours
American food with Dutch specialties

KIEFER'S
105 E. Harmon, 739-8000 ($$) Music
Breakfast, 7:00 AM - 10:00 AM
Dinner, 5:00 PM - 11:00 PM
Friday & Saturday until midnight
Seafood, steaks, veal. View of Strip.

KITCHEN CAFE
4850 W. Flamingo, 222-0880   ($)
8:00 AM - 10:00 PM
Steamed mussels, chicken fra diavolo, pasta

MOUNT CHARLESTON LODGE
Mt. Charleston, 872-5408 ($$) Music
8:00 AM - 10:00 PM
Friday/Saturday until 11:00 PM
Wild mountain platter, duckling

OMELET HOUSE
2160 W. Charleston, 384-6868 ($)
  7:00 AM - 3:00 PM
855 E. Twain, 737-5588
  7:00 AM - 2:00 PM
Homemade soup, omelets, hamburgers, fish

PHILIPS SUPPER HOUSE
4545 W. Sahara, 873-5222 ($$$)
5:00 PM - 11:00 PM
Steaks, seafood, Italian veal, steamed clams

PLANTATION ROOM
Showboat Hotel, 385-9123 ($$)
5:00 PM - 11:00 PM
Spanish paella, porterhouse steak, Cajun catfish

PLAY IT AGAIN SAM
4120 Spring Mountain Rd, 876-1550 ($$) Music
11:00 AM - 5:00 AM
Sunday, 5:00 PM - 2:00 AM
Steak, seafood, crab legs by the pound

POKER PALACE
2757 Las Vegas Blvd. N., 649-9280 ($)
24 Hours
Live whole Maine Lobster, taco salad, steaks

POPPA GAR'S
1624 W. Oakey, 384-4513 ($)
5:00 AM - 9:00 PM
Saturday 5:00 AM - 2:00 PM (Closed Sunday)
Special soups, stuffed hamburger

PORT TACK
3190 W. Sahara, 873-3345 ($$)
11:00 AM - 5:00 AM
Prime steak, fresh fish, salad & oyster bars

RAE'S
Pecos & Wigwam, 897-2000 ($$)
24 Hours
Steaks, steamed clams, ribs, teriyaki chicken

REDWOOD BAR & GRILL
California Hotel, 385-1222 ($$) Music
5:30 PM - 11:00 PM
Friday/Saturday until midnight
Porterhouse steak, mushroom chicken julienne

ROBERTA'S CAFE
El Cortez, 386-0692   ($)
4:30 PM - 10:50 PM
Steaks, seafood, chicken

SADIE'S
505 E. Twain, 796-4177   ($)
11:00 AM - 9:45 PM, Closed Monday
Sunday, 1:00 PM - 7:45 PM
Grits, black-eyed peas, sweet potato pie

SECOND STREET GRILL
Fremont Hotel, 385-6277   ($$$)
6:00 PM - 11:00 PM
Pan-fried crabcakes, veal medallions

SPAGO
Caesars Forum, 369-0360   ($$)
11:00 AM - Midnight
Friday/Saturday until 1:30 AM
Gourmet pizzas, salads, burgers, sandwiches

TONY ROMA'S
Stardust Hotel, 732-6227 ($$)
  5:00 PM - 11:00 PM
  Friday/Saturday until Midnight
Fremont Hotel, 385-3232
  5:00 PM - 11:00 PM
  Friday/Saturday until midnight
620 E. Sahara, 733-9914
  11:00 AM - 10:00 PM
  Friday/Saturday until 10:30 PM
Baby back ribs, onion rings, steak, seafood

WILLIAM B'S
Stardust Hotel, 732-6111 ($$)
5:00 PM - 11:00 PM
Friday/Saturday until midnight
Rib eye steak, chicken or veal kiwi

WOLFGANG PUCK CAFE
MGM Grand, 891-3019   ($$)
11:00 AM - 11:00 PM
Friday - Sunday, 11:00 AM - Midnight
Gourmet pizzas & salads, rotisserie chicken

♥ ♣ ♦ ♠ ♥ ♣ ♦ ♠

* * * GOURMET * * *

ANDRE'S
401 S. Sixth, 385-5016 ($$$)
6:00 PM - 10:30 PM
Classic and nouvelle French specialties, souffles

ANTHONY'S
1550 E. Tropicana, 795-6000   ($$)
Lunch, Monday - Friday, 11:00 AM - 3:00 PM
Dinner, 5:00 PM - 11:00 PM
Friday/Saturday until Midnight, Closed Sunday
Oysters Rockefeller, spinach, gnocchi

ARISTOCRAT
850 S. Rancho, 870-1977 ($$$) Music
Lunch, Monday - Friday, 11:30 AM - 2:00 PM
Dinner, Nightly, 6:00 PM - 10:00 PM
Classique osso bucco, chicken Oscar

BACCHANAL
Caesars Palace, 731-7731 ($$$$) Music
6:00 PM - 10:30 PM
Friday/Saturday seatings, 6:00 PM & 9:30 PM
Closed Sunday & Monday
Fixed-price, seven-course dinner served in
  Roman style, with wines

BISTRO
The Mirage, 791-7111 ($$$$)
6:00 PM - 11:00 PM
Escargot chartreuse, veal loin Montpensier

BUCCANEER BAY CLUB
Treasure Island, 894-7111   ($$$)
5:00 PM - 11:00 PM
Chicken Rossini, tournedos Madeira

BURGUNDY ROOM
Lady Luck Hotel, 477-3000 ($$)
5:00 PM - 11:00 PM
Chicken Rossini, fresh salmon

CAMELOT
Excalibur Hotel, 597-7777 ($$)
6:00 PM - 10:00 PM
Saturday & holidays, 5:00 PM - 11:00 PM
Escargot in brioche, shrimp white knight

DA VINCI'S
Maxim Hotel, 731-4300 ($$)
6:00 PM - 10:30 PM
Veal scallopine, fettuccine Alfredo

HOUSE OF LORDS
Sahara Hotel, 737-2111 ($$$)
6:00 PM - 10:30 PM
Closed Tuesday/Wednesday
Duck salad, steak Diane, frog legs

ISIS
Luxor, 262-4772 ($$$)
5:00 PM - 10:30 PM
Marinated shrimp & lobster, specialty coffees

KELLY & COHEN'S
Vegas World, 382-2000 ($$)
5:00 PM - 11:00 PM
Veal francaise, beef marsala, scampi

LE MONTRACHET
Las Vegas Hilton, 732-5111 ($$$$)
6:00 PM - 10:00 PM, Closed Tuesday
Veal chop stuffed with wild mushrooms

LE PANACHE
Ramada San Remo, 739-9000 ($$$)
5:00 PM - 11:00 PM (Closed Monday/Tuesday)
Beef Wellington, swordfish with lime butter

MICHAEL'S
Barbary Coast Hotel, 737-7111 ($$$$)
Seatings 6:00 PM and 9:00 PM
Rack of lamb bouquetiere, Dover sole

MONTE CARLO ROOM
Desert Inn Hotel, 733-4444 ($$$$)
6:00 PM - 11:00 PM
Closed Tuesday/Wednesday
Hobo steak, stuffed sea bass, veal Normande

PALACE COURT
Caesars Palace, 731-7731 ($$$$) Music
6:00 PM - 11:00 PM
Crevettes flambee, lobster fricassee

PAMPLEMOUSSE
400 E. Sahara, 733-2066 ($$$)
Seatings 6:00 PM & 9:00 PM
Closed Monday
No menu; Waiter recites daily specials

PEGASUS
Alexis Park Hotel, 796-3353 ($$$$) Music
Breakfast, 6:00 AM - 10:00 AM
Lunch, 11:00 AM - 2:30 PM
Dinner, 6:00 PM - 11:00 PM
Duck breast flamed tableside

RENATA'S
4451 E. Sunset, 435-4000 ($$) Music
Lunch, Monday - Friday, 11:00 AM - 3:00 PM
Sunday Champagne Brunch,
   10:00 AM - 3:00 PM
Dinner, Tuesday - Saturday,
   5:00 PM - 11:00 PM
24 Hour Bar Menu
Scampi amoroso, Chinese specialities

SAVOIA
4503 Paradise, 731-5446 **($$)**
Lunch, Monday - Friday, 11:00 AM - 5:00 PM
Dinner, Nightly, 5:00 PM - 10:00 PM
Yucatan duck sausage, hobo steak

SEASONS
Bally's, 739-4651 **($$$$)**
6:00 PM - 11:00 PM
Closed Wednesday/Thursday
Roast duckling Grand Marnier, Chilean sea bass

THE 2ND STORY
4485 S. Jones, 368-2257 **($$)**
6:00 PM - 10:30 PM
Rack of lamb, duck, fresh fish. View of Strip.

SKYE ROOM
Binion's Horseshoe, 382-1600 **($$$)**
6:00 PM - 11:00 PM
Scampi maison, chicken balsam, veal cioppino

SWISS CAFE
1431 E. Charleston, 382-6444 **($$)**
Lunch, Monday - Friday, 11:30 AM - 2:00 PM
Dinner, Tuesday - Saturday, 6:00 PM - 9:15 PM
Veal Zurich, Swiss schnitzel

♥ ♣ ♦ ♠ ♥ ♣ ♦ ♠

* * * ASIAN * * *

AH' SO
Caesars Palace, 731-7331 ($$$$)
6:00 PM - 11:00 PM (Closed Monday)
Six-course, fixed-price dinner in Japanese garden

ASIAN GARDEN
701 N. Nellis Blvd., 453-1900 ($)
11:00 AM - 10:00 PM
Sunday, 4:30 PM - 10:00 PM
Pupu platter, pan-fried spicy shrimp

BAMBOO GARDEN
4850 W. Flamingo, 871-3262 ($$)
11:00 AM - 10:30 PM
Sunday, 5:00 PM - 10:00 PM
Chicken Soong, frog legs Peking style, duck

BENIHANA VILLAGE
Las Vegas Hilton, 732-5111 ($$)
5:00 PM - 11:00 PM
Hibachi tables plus Seafood Grille

CHINA DOLL
2534 E. Desert Inn, 369-9511 ($)
11:00 AM - 10:00 PM
Saturday/Sunday, 3:00 PM - 10:00 PM
Sherry shrimp, steamed whole fish

CHINA FIRST
1801 E. Tropicana, 736-2828   ($$)
4:30 PM - 10:00 PM, Closed Monday
Creamy shrimp soup, sizzling seafood

CHINA ONE
8605 W. Sahara, 254-0328 ($)
Lunch, Tuesday - Friday, 11:30 AM - 3:00 PM
Dinner, 5:00 PM - 10:00 PM
Saturday, Noon - 11:00 PM
Sunday, 3:00 PM - 10:00 PM
Closed Monday
Sizzling rice soup, mu shu shrimp

CHINESE GARDEN
5485 W. Sahara, 876-5432 ($$) Music
11:30 AM - 11:00 PM
Dim Sum until 3:00 PM
Dragon Phoenix soup, lobster tank, no MSG

CHIN'S
3200 Las Vegas Blvd. S., 733-8899 ($$$) Music
11:30 AM - 10:00 PM
Strawberry chicken, Chin's beef, crispy pudding

CHUNG KING
3400 S. Jones, 871-5551 ($$)
11:00 AM - 10:00 PM
Seafood sizzling rice soup, beef in oyster sauce

CHUNG KING II
2801 N. Green Valley Pkwy, 898-2681 ($)
11:00 AM - 10:00 PM
Saturday/Sunday, 4:00 PM - 10:00 PM
Scallops in oyster sauce, sweet & sour duck

DIAMOND CHINESE
2358 Spring Mountain, 796-0103 ($)
11:00 AM - 4:30 AM
Saturday/Sunday, 4:00 PM - 4:00 AM
Hot pot and sizzling platters, chow fun

DRAGON COURT
MGM Grand, 891-7380 ($$)
6:00 PM - 11:00 PM
Seafood wonton soup, orange blossom beef

EMPEROR'S ROOM
Lady Luck Hotel, 477-3000 ($$)
5:00 PM - 11:00 PM/Closed Sunday/Monday
Seaweed with been curd soup, Szechwan shrimp

EMPRESS COURT
Caesars Palace, 731-7110 ($$$$)
6:00 PM - 11:00 PM
Closed Tuesday/Wednesday
Rainbow seafood chowder, Peking duck

GARDEN OF THE DRAGON
Las Vegas Hilton, 732-5111 ($$$)
6:00 PM - 11:00 PM
Abalone with oyster sauce, dungeness crab

GEE JOON
Binion's Horseshoe, 382-1600   ($$)
5:00 PM - 11:00 PM
Mongolian beef, crystal prawns, Peking duck

GEISHA
3751 E. Desert Inn, 451-9814 ($$)
5:00 PM - 10:30 PM (Closed Monday)
Sunday, 5:00 PM - 10:00 PM
Yakitori, tempura, complete hibachi dinners

GOLDEN WOK
4760 S. Eastern, 456-1868 ($$)
11:30 AM - 10:00 PM
Saturday and Sunday, Noon - 10:00 PM
Mandarin, Szechuan, Cantonese

GREAT WALL
Rancho and Charleston, 385-2750 ($)
11:00 AM - 9:30 PM
Saturday, Noon - 9:30 PM
Sunday, 4:00 PM - 9:30 PM
Seaweed soup, gold finger chicken

HAMADA OF JAPAN
598 E. Flamingo, 733-3005 ($$)
5:00 PM - 11:00 PM
Sushi bar (until 2:00 AM)
Teppan grill, sukiyaki dining, yosenabe

HO HO HO
2550 S. Rainbow, 876-6856 ($)
11:00 AM - 10:00 PM
Sunday, 4:00 PM - 10:00 PM
Moo shu pork, kung pao chicken, egg foo young

HOWAN
Desert Inn Hotel, 733-4444 ($$$$)
6:00 PM - 11:00 PM
Prawns in black bean sauce, whole Peking duck

HUNAN KING
5960 Spring Mountain, 221-0456 ($$)
Lunch, 11:30 AM - 3:00 PM
Saturday/Sunday, Noon - 3:00 PM
Dinner, 3:00 PM - 10:00 PM
Kung pao shrimp, Hunan beef, hot & sour soup

KABUKI
1150 E. Twain, 733-0066 ($$)
Lunch, 11:30 AM - 2:00 PM
Dinner, 5:00 PM - 10:00 PM/Closed Sunday
Sushi bar, teriyaki, tempura

KUNG FU PLAZA
3505 S. Valley View, 247-4120   ($$)
11:00 AM - 11:00 PM
Thursday - Saturday until 3:00 AM
Thai crispy catfish

KWEILIN
310 S. Decatur, 870-3889   ($)
11:00 AM - 10:00 PM
Lunch buffet, scallops and lobster

LILLIE LANGTRY'S
Golden Nugget, 385-7111   ($$$$)
5:00 PM - 10:45 PM
Seafood tofu soup, chicken or beef with broccoli

LOTUS OF SIAM
953 E. Sahara, 735-4477   ($$)
Lunch Buffet, Monday - Friday,
   11:30 AM - 2:30 PM
Dinner, Nightly, 4:30 PM - 9:30 PM
Tom Yum seafood soup, Yen Ta Fo noodles

MAYFLOWER CUISINIER
4750 W. Sahara, 870-8432   ($$$)
11:00 AM - 10:00 PM (Friday until 11:00 PM)
Saturday, 5:00 PM - 11:00 PM (Closed Sunday)
Duck dumplings with plum sauce, scallop salad

MIKADO
The Mirage, 791-7111 ($$$$)
6:00 PM - 11:00 PM
Sushi, tempura, hibachi

MING TERRACE
Imperial Palace, 731-3311 ($$)
5:00 PM - 11:00 PM
Abalone, kung pao shrimp, roast duck

MIZUNO'S
Tropicana Hotel, 739-2713 ($$$)
5:00 PM - 10:45 PM
Tempura, Hibachi combination, seafood

MOONGATE
The Mirage, 791-7111 ($$$$)
5:30 PM - 11:00 PM
Filet of salmon Szechwan style, teasmoked duck

NIPPON
101 Convention Center Drive, 735-5565 ($)
Lunch, Monday - Friday, 11:30 AM - 2:00 PM
Dinner, Monday - Saturday,
   6:00 PM - 10:00 PM
Sushi bar, baked scallops, nabe yaki udon

OSAKA
4205 W. Sahara, 876-4988 ($$)
Lunch, Monday - Friday, 11:30 AM - 5:00 PM
Dinner, Nightly, 5:00 PM - 10:00 PM
Friday/Saturday until 11:00 PM
Sushi bar, sukiyaki, donburi mono

PACIFIC RIM
Sahara Hotel, 737-2111 ($$) Music
Seatings 5:30 PM and 8:00 PM
Closed Thursday
Seafood, soup, salad & dessert bar

PAPYRUS
Luxor, 262-4774 ($)
5:00 PM - 10:30 PM
Otemanu hot rock sampler, lemon chicken

PEKING MARKET
Flamingo Hilton, 733-3111 ($$$)
5:30 PM - 10:00 PM
Closed Wednesday/Thursday
Lychee gai, goo lo yuk, kur har

RAINBOW CHINESE CUISINE
1750 S. Rainbow, 877-2211 ($)
11:30 AM - 10:00 PM
Crab and broccoli in wine sauce

RIK' SHAW
Riviera Hotel, 734-5110 ($$)
5:30 PM - 10:45 PM
Closed Wednesday/Thursday
Sung shrimp, pineapple duck

SAIGON
4251 W. Sahara, 362-9978   ($$)
10:00 AM - 10:00 PM
Authentic Vietnamese soup, shrimp

SEOUL KOREAN BBQ
953 E. Sahara, 369-4123   ($)
11:00 AM - 11:00 PM
Crab casserole, broiled adka fish

SILVER DRAGON
1510 E. Flamingo, 737-1234 ($$)
11:30 AM - 5:00 AM
Lover's shrimp, lemon fish, orange beef

SUN SUN
Aladdin, 736-0111   ($$)
5:00 PM - 11:00 PM
Chinese, Vietnamese, Korean specialties

SUSHI BAR SAN REMO
Ramada San Remo, 739-9000 ($$)
6:00 PM - 11:45 PM
Ikura-oroshi, shishamo, unagi, tekka

SUSHI HOUSE MANDA
230 W. Sahara, 382-6006 ($$)
Lunch, Monday - Friday, 11:30 AM - 1:00 PM
Dinner, Nightly, 5:00 PM - 9:30 PM
Friday/Saturday until 11:00 PM
51 kinds of sushi, all you can eat in an hour

SZECHWAN
3101 W. Sahara, 871-4291 ($$)
11:30 AM - 10:30 PM
Fish a la Szechwan, curry chicken

TOKYO
953 E. Sahara, 735-7070 ($$)
Lunch, Monday - Friday, Noon - 2:00 PM
Dinner, Nightly, 5:00 PM - 10:00 PM
Steamed clams with saki, sushi, hibachi, tempura

A TOUCH OF GINGER
4110 S. Maryland Pkwy, 796-1779 ($$)
11:00 AM - 10:00 PM, Closed Sunday
Authentic Vietnamese, imperial rolls

WO FAT
3700 E. Desert Inn, 451-6656 ($)
11:00 AM - 10:00 PM
Clams with black bean sauce, strawberry chicken

♥ ♣ ♦ ♠ ♥ ♣ ♦ ♠

* * * ITALIAN * * *

AL DENTE
Bally's, 739-4111   ($$)
5:30 PM - 11:00 PM, Closed Sunday/Monday
Veal & beef carpaccio, margherita pizza

ALTA VILLA
Flamingo Hilton, 733-3111 ($$)
5:30 PM - 11:00 PM
Minestrone, risotta, veal, pizza

AMICI
6120 W. Tropicana, 222-0380   ($$) Music
Lunch, Monday - Friday, 11:30 AM - 2:30 PM
Dinner, Monday - Saturday,
   5:00 PM - 11:00 PM
Spaghetti puttanesca, gnocchi firenze

ANDIAMO
Las Vegas Hilton, 732-5111 ($$$)
6:00 PM - 11:00 PM
Medaglioni di aragosta, veal chops

ANNABELLA'S
3310 S. Sandhill, 434-2537   ($$)
4:30 PM - 10:30 PM, Closed Monday
Romeo's antipasti, fettuccine with salmon

ANTONIO'S
Rio Suite Hotel, 252-7737 ($$)
5:00 PM - 11:00 PM
Capellini with lobster, cioppino, osso bucco

BATTISTA'S HOLE IN THE WALL
4041 Audrie, 732-1424 ($$) Music
5:00 PM - 11:00 PM
Homemade pasta, veal picante, steak pizzaiola

BERTOLINI'S
Caesars Forum, 735-4663   ($$)
11:30 AM - Midnight
Friday & Saturday until 1:00 AM
Carpaccio alla Cipriani, gourmet pizzas & pastas

BOOTLEGGER RISTORANTE
5025 S. Eastern at Tropicana, 736-4939 ($$)
11:30 AM - 10:30 PM, Closed Monday
Friday & Saturday until 11:00 PM
Sunday, 4:00 PM - 10:00 PM
Lobster-seafood diablo, veal piccata

CAFE MILANO
3900 Paradise, 732-2777 ($$)
Lunch, Monday - Friday, 11:00 AM - 3:00 PM
Dinner, Monday - Saturday,
   5:00 PM - 10:00 PM (Closed Sunday)
Fettuccine pomodora, penne arabiata

CARLUCCIO'S TIVOLI GARDENS
1775 E. Tropicana, 795-3236 ($) Music
4:30 PM - 10:00 PM (Closed Monday)
Veal florentine, stuffed shrimp, seafood diablo

CHE PASTA
2801 Athenian Dr., Henderson, 435-0036   ($)
Lunch, Tuesday - Friday, 11:00 AM - 2:30 PM
Dinner, 5:00 PM - 10:00 PM, Closed Monday
Eggplant cannelloni, veal sausage dijonnaise

CHIASSO CAFE
4712 W. Sahara, 877-2870   ($)
11:00 AM - 10:00 PM (Closed Monday)
Friday/Saturday until 11:00 PM
Pizzas, pastas, veal Marsala

CHICAGO JOE'S
820 S. Fourth, 382-5637 ($$)
Lunch, Monday - Friday, 11:00 AM - 5:00 PM
Dinner, Monday - Saturday,
   5:00 PM - 10:00 PM
Chicago hot shrimp, linguine with calamari

CHICAGO JOE'S HIDEAWAY
8101 W. Racel, 645-7201   ($$)
5:00 PM - 10:00 PM, Sunday until 9:30 PM
Closed Monday
Pasta, steaks, veal picante, chicken vesuvio

CIPRIANI
2790 E. Flamingo, 369-6711 ($$$)
Lunch, Monday - Friday, 11:00 AM - 2:30 PM
Dinner, Monday - Saturday,
   5:30 PM - 10:30 PM
Steamed clams in white wine, chicken Abruzzese

DI MARTINO'S
Tropicana Hotel, 739-2341   ($$$)
5:00 PM - 11:00 PM
Baked mozzarella on tomato sauce

DI NAPOLI
Showboat Hotel, 385-9123 ($$)
5:00 PM - 11:00 PM
Sunday Family Feast, 2:00 PM - 11:00 PM
Freshly made pastas, lobster fra diavolo

FERRARO'S
5900 W. Flamingo, 364-5300 ($$) Music
5:30 PM - 10:30 PM
Frittura di calamari, stuffed artichoke

FORTUNATO'S
3430 E. Tropicana, 458-3333 ($$)
11:00 AM - 10:00 PM
Sunday, 4:00 PM - 10:00 PM
Saltimbocca, gnocchi, cioppino

LANCE-A-LOTTA PASTA
Excalibur Hotel, 597-7777 ($) Music
Lunch, 11:00 AM - 2:30 PM
Dinner, 5:00 PM - 10:00 PM
Friday/Saturday/Holidays until Midnight
Antipasto, pastas, eggplant Parmesan, tartufo

LA STRADA
4640 Paradise, 735-0150 ($$) Music
5:00 PM - 11:00 PM
Mussels peasant style, calamari provencale

LA TERRAZZA
Sahara Hotel, 737-2111 ($$)
5:30 PM - 10:30 PM (Closed Sunday/Monday)
Pollo Tonato, Timbale Toscano, lobster

LEONARDO'S
MGM Grand, 891-7331   ($$)
Lunch, 11:00 AM - 3:00 PM
Dinner, 6:00 PM - 11:00 PM
Northern Italian, pizzas, antipasto bar, pastas

MANFREDI'S LIMELIGHT
2340 E. Tropicana, 739-1410 ($$) Music
4:30 PM - 9:00 PM (Closed Sunday)
Friday/Saturday until 10:00 PM
Agnolotti, linguine tutto mare

NEW YORK PASTA CO.
Hacienda Hotel, 891-8285   ($$)
5:00 PM - 10:30 PM
Pizzas, veal Marsala, chicken cacciatore

NORTH BEACH CAFE
2605 S. Decatur, 247-9530   ($$) Music
Lunch, Monday - Friday, 11:30 AM - 5:00 PM
Dinner, 5:00 PM - 9:30 PM (Closed Sunday)
Friday/Saturday, 5:00 PM - 10:00 PM
Insalata caprese, chicken cognac, agnolotti

OLIVE GARDEN
1545 E. Flamingo, 735-0082 ($)
1361 S. Decatur, 258-3453
6850 W. Cheyenne, 658-2144
11:00 AM - 10:00 PM
Friday/Saturday until 11:00 PM
Brick oven pizza, homemade garlic breadsticks

PASTA MIA
2585 E. Flamingo, 733-0091 ($$)
   Noon - 9:30 PM
4455 W. Flamingo, 251-8871
   11:00 AM - 10:00 PM
   Sunday, Noon - 10:00 PM
Creative pastas, antipasto freddo

PASTA PALACE
Palace Station, 367-2411 ($)
5:00 PM - 11:00 PM
Linguine, spaghetti, Italian salad, veals

PASTA PIRATE
California Hotel, 385-1222 ($)
5:30 PM - 11:00 PM
Sesame lobster brochettes, Cajun tuna

PASTA REMO
Ramada San Remo, 739-9000 ($)
4:00 PM - Midnight
Steamed clams, calamari, agnolotti, cannelloni

PASTA SHOP
2495 E. Tropicana, 451-1893 ($$)
5:00 PM - 9:00 PM (Closed Sunday)
Friday/Saturday until 9:30 PM
Homemade pastas, Caesar salad, chicken Davida

PIERO'S
355 Convention Center Dr., 369-2305 ($$$)
5:30 PM - 10:30 PM
Cozze in brodetto, veal chop in brandy sauce

PIZZA PALACE
Imperial Palace, 731-3311 ($)
11:00 AM - Midnight
Pizzas, sandwiches, Italian mini-feasts

PORTOFINO
Desert Inn Hotel, 733-4444 ($$$$)
6:00 PM - 11:00 PM, Closed Sunday/Monday
Pollo alla Romano, whole New England lobster

PRIMAVERA
Caesars Palace, 731-7731 ($$$)
Breakfast, 9:00 AM - 11:00 AM
Lunch, Noon - 3:00 PM
Dinner, 6:00 PM - 11:00 PM
Ravioli Mario, swordfish with artichokes

RISTORANTE ITALIANO
Riviera Hotel, 734-5110 ($$)
5:30 PM - 11:00 PM, Closed Monday/Tuesday
Vermicelli salsa bella vista, lobster francaise

RIVA
The Mirage, 791-7111 ($$$$)
6:00 PM - 11:00 PM
Pasta e fagioli, gnocchi della casa

ROMEO'S
2800 W. Sahara, 873-5400 ($$$) Music
Lunch, Monday - Friday, 11:00 AM - 2:00 PM
Dinner, Nightly, 5:00 PM - 10:00 PM
Friday/Saturday until 10:30 PM
Carpaccio, fettuccine con salmone

RUFINO'S
1640 Warm Springs Rd., 456-2520   ($$)
Lunch, Monday - Friday, 11:00 AM - 3:00 PM
Sunday Brunch, 9:00 AM - 2:00 PM
Dinner, Nightly, 5:00 PM - 10:00 PM
Chicken Joann, veal Wisconsin, pizzaiola steak

SERGIO'S
1955 E. Tropicana, 739-1544   ($$)   Music
Lunch, Monday - Friday, 11:30 AM - 2:30 PM
Dinner, Nightly, 5:30 PM - 11:00 PM
Linguini with Maine lobster, veal St. Moritz

SICILIAN CAFE
3510 E. Tropicana, 456-1300   ($$)
Cafe:
  Lunch, Monday - Friday, 11:30 AM - 4:00 PM
  Dinner, Nightly, 4:00 PM - 10:30 PM
Restaurant:
  5:00 PM - 10:00 PM
Linguine pescatore, chicken braciola and scampi

STEFANO'S
Golden Nugget, 385-7111   ($$$)
6:00 PM - 11:00 PM
Cappellini frutti di mare, cioppino

THAT'S ITALIAN
4601 W. Sahara, 873-8055   ($$)
5:30 PM - 9:30 PM   (Closed Sunday)
Veal Angelo, shrimp fradiavolo, chicken Luciano

VENETIAN
3713 W. Sahara, 876-4190 **($$)**
4:00 PM - 11:00 PM
Homemade pastas, provimi veal, fresh fish

VERN ELLER'S
3715 S. Decatur, 362-7991   **($)** Music
5:00 PM - 11:00 PM / Sunday until 10:00 PM
Steaks, prime rib, veal gran duca, fresh fish

VESUVIO
1020 E. Desert Inn, 735-1170   **($$)**
5:00 PM - 10:00 PM
Fresh Florida stone crab, cioppino

VICTORIA'S
6135 W. Sahara, 222-1809   **($$)**
Lunch, Monday - Friday, 11:30 AM - 4:00 PM
Dinner, Nightly, 4:00 PM - 10:00 PM
Angel hair with scallops marinara, scampi

VINCENZO RISTORANTE
610 E. Naples, 737-5755   **($$)**
4:00 PM - 11:00 PM
Giombota, mussels fra diavolo, veal Siciliano

VINEYARD
Boulevard Mall, 731-1606 **($$)**
11:00 AM - 10:00 PM
Friday/Saturday until 11:00 PM
Salad bar with fresh-baked bread, pizza, soup

*** MEXICAN/SOUTHWESTERN ***

ANASAZI
Vacation Village Hotel, 897-1700 ($)
24 Hours
Sizzling fajitas, orange roughy La Pacifica

BRINK'S CRAZY CANTINA
2850 E. Tropicana, 456-3023 ($)
9:00 AM - 10:00 PM
Friday until 11:00 PM / Sunday until 9:00 PM
Chicken, shrimp, beef, fish and pork fajitas

CHAPALAS
3335 E. Tropicana, 451-8141 ($)
  11:00 AM - Midnight
2101 S. Decatur, 871-1915
  11:00 AM - 11:00 PM
  Friday/Saturday until Midnight)
Pork ensalada Grampa, chilaquiles con chorizo

COYOTE CAFE
MGM Grand, 891-7347
Cafe ($$):
  9:00 AM - Midnight
  Appetizers, casseroles, salads, soups, tacos
Restaurant ($$$):
  Lunch, 11:30 AM - 2:30 PM
  Dinner, 5:30 PM - 11:00 PM
  Mark Miller's sizzling painted soup

DONA MARIA
910 Las Vegas Blvd. South, 382-6538 ($)
8:00 AM - 11:00 PM
Fresh tamales, burritos, enchiladas, chili relleno

EL BURRITO WEST
633 N. Decatur, 870-1969 ($)
11:00 AM - 9:45 PM
Friday/Saturday until 10:45 PM
Sunday, Noon - 9:45 PM
Special soft taco, machaca, Mexican steak

EL SOMBRERO
807 S. Main, 382-9234 ($)
11:00 AM - 10:30 PM, Closed Sunday
Menudo soup, chili Colorado, natillas

GARCIA'S
1030 E. Flamingo, 731-0628 ($)
11:00 AM - 10:00 PM
Friday/Saturday until 11:00 PM
Chimichangas, tostadas, enchiladas

GUADALAJARA BAR & GRILLE
Palace Station, 367-2411 ($$)
Lunch, 11:00 AM - 5:00 PM
Dinner, 5:00 PM - 11:00 PM
Steak Especiale, tacos al carbon

LA SALSA TAQUERIA/CANTINA
Caesars Forum, 735-8226   ($)
  11:00 AM - 11:00 PM
  Friday/Saturday until Midnight
  Sunday until 10:30 PM
Boulevard Mall
  10:00 AM - 9:00 PM
  Saturday, 10:00 AM - 6:00 PM
  Sunday, 11:00 AM - 6:00 PM
Gourmet chicken burritos, pollo asada

LAS OLAS
Bally's, 739-4111   ($$$)   Music
5:30 PM - 11:30 PM
Enchiladas, fajitas, sopaipillas

LINDO MICHOACAN
2655 E. Desert Inn, 735-6828   ($)
11:00 AM - 10:00 PM
Friday/Saturday until 11:00 PM
Sunday, 10:00 AM - 10:00 PM
Chicken with cactus, shrimp with verde sauce

MACAYO
1741 E. Charleston, 382-5605 ($)
4457 W. Charleston, 878-7347
1375 E. Tropicana, 736-1898
11:00 AM - Midnight
Fajitas, tamales, chimichangas, chili relleno

MARGARITA'S CANTINA
Frontier Hotel, 794-8200 ($)
11:00 AM - 10:30 PM
Carne asada, pollo fajitas

MARGARITAVILLE
Las Vegas Hilton, 732-5111 ($$)
5:00 PM - 11:00 PM, Closed Wednesday
Flautas, fajitas, margarita pie

PAISANO'S
2210 Paradise, 731-4877 ($)
11:00 AM - 11:00 PM
Saturday/Sunday, 5:00 PM - 11:00 PM
Enchiladas rancheras, chile verde burrito

RICARDO'S
2380 E. Tropicana, 798-4515 ($$) Music
  11:00 AM - 11:00 PM
  Friday/Saturday until Midnight
  Sunday, Noon - 10:00 PM
4930 W. Flamingo, 871-7119
  11:00 AM - 11:00 PM
  Sunday, Noon - 10:00 PM
4300 Meadows Lane, 870-1088
  11:00 AM - 10:00 PM
  Friday/Saturday until 11:00 PM
  Sunday until 8:00 PM
Steak picado, carne asada

SOMBRERO ROOM
Binion's Horseshoe, 382-1600 ($)
4:00 PM - 11:00 PM
Fajitas, tostados, enchiladas

THREE AMIGOS
6250 Mountain Vista, 435-3322 ($$)
11:00 AM - 10:00 PM
Friday/Saturday until 11:00 PM
Broccoli burrito, chile verde, pork carnitas

TRES LOBOS
Stardust Hotel, 732-6111 ($)
5:00 PM - 11:00 PM
Friday/Saturday until Midnight
Steak Lobos, crab & shrimp enchiladas, steaks

VIVA MERCADO'S
6182 W. Flamingo, 871-8826 ($)
11:00 AM - 10:00 PM
Friday/Saturday until 11:00 PM
Quesadillas, steak azada, taquitos dorados

WILLY & JOSE'S
Sam's Town, 454-8044 ($)
4:00 PM - 10:00 PM
Friday/Saturday until 11:00 PM
Enchiladas, flautas, steak picado

♥ ♣ ♦ ♠ ♥ ♣ ♦ ♠

* * * STEAKS * * *

ALL-AMERICAN BAR & GRILLE
Rio Suite Hotel, 252-7767 ($$)
Lunch, 11:00 AM - 5:00 PM
Dinner, 5:00 PM - 11:00 PM
Mesquite-grilled steaks and seafood, pork ribs

BALLY'S STEAKHOUSE
Bally's Hotel, 739-4661 ($$$$)
6:00 PM - 11:00 PM
Cajun-grilled shrimp cocktail, lobster

BEEF BARRON
Flamingo Hilton, 733-3502 ($$$)
5:30 PM - 11:30 PM, Closed Monday/Tuesday
Steaks, lobster, prime rib, Texas caviar

BINIONS' RANCH
Horseshoe Hotel, 382-1600 ($$)
5:00 PM - 10:45 PM
Chopped sirloin, New York, porterhouse

BOB TAYLOR'S RANCH HOUSE
Rio Vista Street near U.S. 95, 645-1399 ($$)
5:30 PM - 8:30 PM (Closed Monday)
Friday/Saturday until 9:30 PM
Steaks, chicken, lamb chops, seafood

BUFFALO RANCH
577 E. Sahara, 732-3656   ($$)
Lunch, Monday - Friday, 11:00 AM - 4:00 PM
   Saturday, Noon - 4:00 PM
Dinner, Nightly, 4:00 PM - 10:00 PM
Friday/Saturday until 11:00 PM
Buffalo burgers, smoked prime rib, fresh trout

DIAMOND LIL'S
Sam's Town, 456-7777   ($$)
5:30 PM - 10:00 PM, Closed Monday/Tuesday
Friday/Saturday until 11:00 PM
Sunday Champagne Brunch, 9:30 AM - 2:30 PM
Grilled oysters, fresh fish, rack of lamb

EL GAUCHO
Tropicana Hotel, 739-2222   ($$)
5:00 PM - 10:30 PM
Oysters del Rio, swordfish Mazatlan

EMBERS
Imperial Palace, 731-3311   ($$)
5:00 PM - 11:00 PM, Closed Monday/Tuesday
Oysters Embers, scallop fettuccine Alfredo

GOLDEN STEER
308 W. Sahara, 384-4470   ($$$)
5:00 PM - Midnight
Prime rib, seafood, game birds

HARRINGTON'S
4760 W. Sahara, 878-7374   ($$)
Lunch, Monday - Saturday, 11:00 AM - 3:30 PM
Dinner, Nightly, 5:00 PM - 11:00 PM
Coquille St. Jacques, New York steak, swordfish

HILTON STEAKHOUSE
Las Vegas Hilton, 732-5111   ($$$)
5:00 PM - 11:00 PM, Closed Thursday
Steaks, swordfish, lemon oregano chicken

HUGO'S CELLAR
Four Queens Hotel, 385-4011   ($$$)
6:00 PM - 10:30 PM
Steaks, seafood, shrimp, salad cart

HUNGRY HUNTER
2380 S. Rainbow, 873-0433   ($$)
Lunch, Monday - Saturday, 11:00 AM - 3:00 PM
Dinner, 5:00 PM - 10:00 PM
Friday/Saturday until 11:00 PM
Sunday, 4:00 PM - 10:00 PM
Lemon-herb chicken, whiskey peppercorn steak

KRISTOFER'S
Riviera Hotel, 794-9233   ($$$)
5:30 PM - 11:00 PM
Steaks, chops, swordfish, complimentary dessert

LONE STAR
1290 E. Flamingo, 893-0348 ($$)
1611 S. Decatur, 259-0105
11:00 AM - 10:00 PM
Thursday - Saturday until 11:00 PM
Amarillo cheese fries, Texas tumbleweed

MORTON'S
Fashion Show Mall, 893-0703   ($$$$)
5:00 PM - 11:00 PM, Sunday until 10:00 PM
Seafood, black bean soup, steaks, prime rib

PALM
Caesars Forum, 732-7256   ($$$$)
11:30 AM - 11:00 PM
Steaks, chops, crab cakes, veal, pasta

RUTH'S CHRIS STEAK HOUSE
3900 Paradise, 791-7011 ($$$$)
4561 W. Flamingo
4:30 PM - 11:30 PM
New York strip, veal chop, salmon fillet

SIR REGINALD STEAKHOUSE
MGM Grand, 891-7318   ($$$)
6:00 PM - 11:00 PM
Gravlax, hobo steak, rack of lamb

THE STEAK HOUSE
Circus Circus Hotel, 734-0410 ($$)
5:00 PM - Midnight
Open grill for filet, New York, T-bone steaks

WILD BILL'S
Excalibur, 597-7777   ($$) Music
5:00 PM - 10:00 PM
Friday/Saturday until 11:00 PM
Cat Ballou catfish, buckshot chili

YOLIE'S
3900 Paradise, 794-0700 ($$)
Lunch, Monday - Friday, 11:00 AM - 3:00 PM
Dinner, Nightly, 5:30 PM - 10:00 PM
Friday/Saturday until 11:00 PM
Brazilian price-fixed mesquite-broiled banquet

♥ ♣ ♦ ♠ ♥ ♣ ♦ ♠

* * * SEAFOOD * * *

BUZIOS
Rio Suite Hotel, 252-7777 ($$$)
11:00 AM - 11:00 PM
Steamers, chowders, seafood pastas, cioppino

DICKINSON'S WHARF
957 E. Sahara, 732-3594 ($$)
5:00 PM - 11:00 PM
Live Maine lobster, steaks, Italian specialties

FAMOUS PACIFIC FISH COMPANY
3925 Paradise, 796-9676 ($$)
Lunch, Monday - Saturday, 11:00 AM - 4:00 PM
Dinner, Nightly, 4:00 PM - 10:00 PM
Friday/Saturday until 11:00 PM
Fresh fish, seafood chowder, mussels

FISHERMAN'S BROILER
Palace Station, 367-2411 ($$)
Lunch, 11:00 AM - 4:00 PM
   Saturday/Sunday, Noon - 4:00 PM
Dinner, 4:00 PM - 11:00 PM
   Friday/Saturday until 11:30 PM
Salmon, halibut and other fresh varieties

FISHERMAN'S PORT
Aladdin Hotel, 736-0111 ($$$)
5:00 PM - 11:00 PM
Steamed clams, crab or lobster francaise

KOKOMO'S
The Mirage, 791-7111 ($$$)
Lunch, 11:30 AM - 3:00 PM
Dinner, 5:30 PM - 11:30 PM
Scallops in potato crust, lamb chops

MEDITERRANEAN ROOM
Gold Coast Hotel, 367-7111 ($$)
5:00 PM - 11:00 PM
Swordfish, cioppino, veal picante

NEROS
Caesars Palace, 731-7731 ($$$) Music
5:30 PM - 10:30 PM
Maine lobster, prime rib-eye, prime steaks, flan

OCEAN GRILLE
MGM Grand, 891-7319 ($$)
Lunch, 11:00 AM - 3:00 PM
Dinner, 6:00 PM - 11:00 PM
Sauteed soft shell crab, grilled yellow tail

RED LOBSTER
2323 E. Flamingo, 731-0119 ($)
200 S. Decatur, 877-0212
11:00 AM - 10:00 PM
Friday/Saturday until 11:00 PM
Broiled fisherman's platter, steak and lobster

ROSEWOOD GRILLE
3339 Las Vegas Boulevard S., 792-9099 ($$$$)
4:30 PM - 11:30 PM
Prime rib, Main lobster, Florida stone crab

SACRED SEA ROOM
Luxor, 262-4772   ($$)
5:00 PM - 10:30 PM
Scallops with plum soy garlic sauce

ST. THOMAS SEAFOOD GROTTO
Frontier Hotel, 794-8240 ($$)
Breakfast, 8:00 AM - Noon
Lunch, Noon - 2:30 PM
Dinner, 5:00 PM - 10:00 PM
Friday/Saturday until 11:00 PM
Salmon fettuccine, teriyaki ahi, thresher shark

STARBOARD TACK
2601 Atlantic, 457-8794 ($$)
11:00 AM - Midnight, Friday until 2:00 AM
Saturday, 5:00 PM - 2:00 AM
Sunday, 5:00 PM - Midnight
Appetizers, steaks, steamed clams, fresh oysters

TILLERMAN
2245 E. Flamingo, 731-4036 ($$$)
5:00 PM - 11:00 PM
Catch of the day, shrimp, lobster

♥ ♣ ♦ ♠ ♥ ♣ ♦ ♠

* * * SPECIALTY * * *

ALPINE VILLAGE INN (GERMAN)
3003 Paradise, 734-6888 ($$) Music
5:00 PM - 11:00 PM
Chicken Supreme soup, sauerbraten

BARRONSHIRE (ENGLISH)
Las Vegas Hilton, 732-5801 ($$$)
6:00 PM - 10:30 PM, Closed Wednesday
Cuts of prime rib, chicken, seafood

JOE'S BAYOU (CAJUN)
Harrah's, 369-5000 ($$)
5:00 PM - 11:00 PM (Tuesday until 10:00 PM)
Bayou sampler, Louisiana gumbo, blackened fish

**MAD DOG'S AND ENGLISHMEN PUB
 (ENGLISH)**
4755 Spring Mountain, 362-0074 ($) Music
515 Las Vegas Blvd. S., 382-5075
11:00 AM - 10:00 PM
Fish & chips, Cornish pastie, bangers & mash

**MIDDLE EASTERN BAZAAR
 (MIDDLE EAST)**
4147 S. Maryland Pkwy., 731-6030 ($)
Monday - Friday, 10:00 AM - 7:00 PM
Saturday, 11:00 AM - 5:00 PM
Falafel, grape leaves, hummus, kosher products

OLD HEIDELBERG (GERMAN)
604 E. Sahara, 731-5310 ($$)
10:00 AM - 6:00 PM, Closed Sunday
Friday/Saturday until 8:00 PM
Veal bratwurst, knockwurst, soups, apple strudel

OLYMPIC CAFE (GREEK)
4023 Spring Mountain, 876-7900 ($$)
Lunch, Monday - Friday, 11:00 AM - 4:00 PM
Dinner, 5:00 PM - 10:00 PM
Friday/Saturday until 11:00 PM/Closed Sunday
Hot and cold pikilia, chicken sauvlaki

RED SEA (ETHIOPIAN)
2226 Paradise, 893-1741 ($)
11:00 AM - 10:30 PM
Sambusa, hummus, vegetarian specialities

SIR GALAHAD'S (ENGLISH)
Excalibur Hotel, 597-7777 ($$)
5:00 PM - 10:00 PM
Friday/Saturday until Midnight
Holiday until 11:00 PM
Seafood crepes Neptune, prime rib, trifle

♥ ♣ ♦ ♠ ♥ ♣ ♦ ♠

CHURCHES

It has been said that Las Vegas has more churches per capita than any other city in the United States. We're not sure if that is a proven fact, but below is a listing of the type of churches found in Las Vegas, and the number of each found in our area. A complete listing with the individual church name, address, and phone number can be found in the telephone book yellow pages. The members of our various churches are known to be helpful, caring and generous people. Some wonderful friendships can be made there. Since Las Vegas is a 24-hour town, many of the churches have several services, and on various days, to accommodate our 24-hour residents. They make it easy for you to attend, and most services are well-attended.

    African Methodist Episcopal (1)
    Anglican (1)
    Apostolic (11)
    Assemblies of God (10)
    Baha'i (2)

Baptist (79) These include American, Bible Fellowship, Conservative, G.A.R.B.C., Independent, Independent-Fundamental, Missionary and Southern Baptist.
Bible (2)
Buddhist (2)
Catholic (27) These include Byzantine and Latin Rite Catholic Churches
Christian (9)
Christian Science (3)
Church of Christ (13)
Church of God (10)
Church of God in Christ (16)
Church of God of Prophecy (1)
Church of Jesus Christ of Latter Day Saints (Mormon) - Approximately 80 wards
Church of Religious Science (2)
Community (2)
Episcopal (7)
Evangelical - Free (1)
Foursquare Gospel (7)
Full Gospel (4)
Independent Bible (2)
Inter-Denominational (12)
Jehovah's Witnesses (5)

Lutheran (19)
Metropolitan Community (1)
Muhammed's Temple (1)
Nazarene (3)
Non-Denominational (38)
Open Bible (1)
Orthodox Eastern (5)
Pentecostal (11)
Presbyterian (9)
Religious Science (6)
Salvation Army (2)
Science of Mind (3)
Scientology (1)
Seventh-Day Adventists (4)
Unitarian Universalist (1)
United Church of Christ (2)
United Methodist (13)
United Pentecostal (1)
Unity (1)
Universology (1)
Various Denominations (2)

As you can see, Las Vegas has well over 400 churches in its midst. To find one that satisfies your religious and personal beliefs should be relatively easy. You may want to talk with your hometown pastor/priest and acquire his suggestions as to the church to attend. Oftentimes, the hometown pastor or priest has had occasion to meet his Las Vegas counterpart and would be willing to write a letter to introduce you. Your church leaders may often provide helpful information that you may require upon arrival in Las Vegas.

****

From the loudspeaker of a female liberationists' convention came this announcement: "God made Adam for practice. Then he looked him over and said, "I think I can do better than that." So he made Eve.

♥ ♣ ♦ ♠ ♥ ♣ ♦ ♠

LAS VEGAS AND ITS "SUBURBS"

Las Vegas became a city in 1905. In 1931, when gambling was legalized in Nevada, Hoover Dam was also being built, so the population saw a hefty increase. The downtown area of Las Vegas became the gambling mecca as casinos were built along Fremont Street. In 1940, the first "Strip" hotel was built. It was named the El Rancho. Shortly thereafter, the Flamingo Hotel joined the El Rancho on the Strip, and the rest is history. Today there are over 50,000 hotel rooms lining Las Vegas Boulevard, better known as "The Strip", and by 1994, there will be at least 10,000 more.

There are various areas of Las Vegas that have their own townships such as Spring Valley, Paradise Valley, Sunrise Manor, and Winchester. However, their city address is still Las Vegas. There are also adjoining sections which do use their own city address, which include North Las Vegas and Henderson. Henderson also incorporates the Green Valley area. Boulder City is approximately 30 miles southeast of Las Vegas and is a green and picturesque little town near Hoover Dam and Lake Mead. Boulder City is known to host a bevy of cultural events throughout the year, and the residents of Las Vegas flock to that beautiful little city to participate.

Approximately two hours southeast of Las Vegas on the Nevada/Arizona border you will find the fastest growing gaming city in Nevada - Laughlin. That village, which had approximately 100 residents in 1984, now has about 5000. There are ten hotels in the area at the present time, with others under construction. The town is situated on the Colorado River directly across from Bullhead City, Arizona. It reminds one of the early days of Las Vegas with its rapid growth, becoming an oasis in the barren desert.

Mt. Charleston and Lee Canyon are approximately 35 miles west of Las Vegas. This is another beautiful area which has grown tremendously in the last few years. More and more people are building homes and cabins in the high mountain area. It is a wonderful place to enjoy cool summer temperatures and great skiing in the winter.

The Mt. Charleston Hotel is located at the foot of the Mountains with stables for horseback riding. Toward the top of the mountain, nestled away in the tall pines, is a large lodge which serves breakfast, lunch, and dinner. They offer sleigh rides in the winter, and in their lounge is a cozy fireplace by which skiers can snuggle. Many local Las Vegans sneak up there in the summer to escape the heat in the city. That large log cabin is called the Mt. Charleston Lodge...a great get-away for summer or winter.

****

The residents of Las Vegas were asked what they considered to be the best tourist attraction to take their out-of-town guests. They overwhelmingly voted the "Las Vegas Strip". One clever newspaperman added his favorite place to take them..."to the airport".

♥ ♣ ♦ ♠ ♥ ♣ ♦ ♠

NELLIS AIR FORCE BASE

Nellis Air Force Base is located approximately eight miles northeast of downtown Las Vegas, and encompasses about 37,000 people who are part of a military family. The base employs over 13,000 people, making it the single largest employer in Southern Nevada. The total land area of the base, including the restricted training ranges, covers approximately 4700 square miles. The USAF Demonstration Squadron is widely known throughout the United States, most recognizable by the name "Thunderbirds". Every year a large air show is given at Nellis Air Force Base, and people come from hundreds of miles away to see the large assortment of aircraft, and the spectacular feats accomplished by the Thunderbirds and other flyers. An exceptionally large viewing audience came to the show in 1990 to get a first-hand look at the new Stealth Fighter.

Many of the Nellis personnel, as well as many civilians, are employed at the Nevada Test Site. The Test Site is approximately 50 miles northwest of Las Vegas and is a high security government installation. A great deal of top secret projects are developed and tested there. There are persistent rumors of

UFO sightings in that entire region, but as that area is off-limits to civilians, questions about the sightings are left unanswered. You can be sure, however, that much of the high technology and strategy that was used during the Persian Gulf crisis was developed right here in Nevada at the Test Site and at Nellis Air Force Base. Although large sections of Nevada appear to be a huge desert wasteland, the State of Nevada plays an invaluable role in the needs of the U.S. Government. In other words, we are a very important little state, and we have much to be proud of!

    All of Las Vegas gave a royal "Welcome Home" to our troops when they returned from the Persian Gulf. During the crisis, there was a large outpouring of emotional and financial support offered to the families of the troops by the Las Vegas residents. The people of Las Vegas have always proven to be very generous, caring and patriotic.

♥ ♣ ♦ ♠ ♥ ♣ ♦ ♠

WINNING IN LAS VEGAS

When Frances and her husband moved to Las Vegas, it was a whole new experience. The only gambling Frances had ever done was playing penny ante poker with her relatives back home. Her husband found a job on the second day they were in town, so there had been no opportunity to see what this gambling city had to offer. When her cousin called and offered to take her, she was anxious to go. They went to the Stardust Hotel where Frances was introduced to a game called keno. Her cousin explained the game and instructed Frances to mark the keno ticket with "X's". She picked eight numbers. When the drawn numbers began flashing on the board, she had seven out of eight, which meant she had won about $1200. It was the very first gambling Frances had ever done in this town, and she couldn't believe how easy it was.

It has been sixteen years since Frances moved here, and although she doesn't do much gambling, she still enjoys going out once in awhile to "donate" her $20....or perhaps win $40 or $50....whichever the case may be. Bingo, which is something similar to keno, has now become her favorite game. She said that in bingo she can go in to play with only $6.00

and play for an hour. In keno, at $1.00 a ticket, $6.00 can be gone in thirty minutes. Another reason that bingo now appeals to her is that in the past sixteen years, this lucky lady has managed to win $1000 at least sixteen times. At this point, however, it is only fair to tell you about another woman I know who has lived here for six years. She has gone to play bingo at least once a month for the past six years, and has yet to win even one of those $1000 games!

****

People who go through life keeping their fingers crossed usually end up with nothing more than sore fingers!

♥ ♣ ♦ ♠ ♥ ♣ ♦ ♠

RECREATION

People with children often hesitate when considering Las Vegas as a place to settle. They think of Las Vegas as an "adult" city. They never stop to consider that there is a whole different life in Las Vegas beyond the Las Vegas Strip. The residents of Las Vegas entertain themselves the same way residents of other cities do.

We have little league baseball, children's soccer, football and basketball, 4-H Clubs, Boys and Girls Clubs of America, YMCA, swimming, tennis, miniature golf, bicycling, bowling, water skiing, snow skiing, fishing, movie theaters, pizza parlors, dance classes, gymnast clubs, roller skating, ice skating (year round), and the list goes on and on. The Lied Discovery Children's Museum has been a place of total fascination for Las Vegas youngsters. Once they have gone there, they want to return often. Three hotels in Las Vegas - Circus Circus, Excalibur, and the MGM Grand - offer a huge variety of child and teen entertainment on a daily basis. In the summer, there is the Wet 'N Wild theme park. Caesars Palace offers the Omnimax Theater which is a big hit with kids as well as adults. There are so many other things for kids to become involved in that they could be kept very busy in Las Vegas.

The adults in Las Vegas have an abundance of entertainment and recreational activities available to them. Much of what is listed under the children's recreational activities applies to adults also. Golf, tennis, bowling, racquetball, softball, movie theaters, and bingo seem to have top priorities here, along with a host of water sports, including swimming, fishing, and boating. There are many cultural events going on weekly in stage, theater, music, dance and art, all of which are well attended.

Las Vegas has fast become a city where gambling isn't the only recreation available. Our beautiful desert landscaping and magnificent mountains will invite you for a look, as will the Hoover Dam/Lake Mead area. The following is a listing of some pretty areas for recreation and relaxation.

FLOYD R. LAMB STATE PARK
(486-5413)

Located ten miles north of Las Vegas off U.S. 95 at Tule Springs, this park reflects many phases of development in Southern Nevada history. Picnic facilities are offered, along with self-guided walking trails through tree-shaded groves and along small lakes.

LAKE MEAD NATIONAL RECREATION AREA
(293-8920)

The Alan Bible Visitor's Center is the single best source of information on the recreational area. The Center contains a botanical garden and exhibits on natural history.

MT. CHARLESTON RECREATION AREA
(872-7098)

This mountain playground, located 35 miles northwest of Las Vegas on U.S. 95, offers something for everyone. Visitors can enjoy picnicking, hiking, and sightseeing. The Spring Mountain scenic loop is a favorite of visitors. Favorite winter activities include skiing, sledding and sleigh rides. The rustic lodges welcome you with open arms and good food.

RED ROCK CANYON
(363-1921)

The Bureau of Land Management's Red Rock Canyon National Conservation Area is located 15 miles west of Las Vegas off West Charleston Boulevard. This place is nature at its best because it is the home of the Red Rock Escarpment, a 3000-foot high mass of multicolored pinnacles and boulders jutting from the canyon floor. It will take your breath away. While driving along the 13-mile scenic loop drive, you will be surprised by the wild burros which come right up to your car. Picnic areas and hiking trails are also available. This truly is a must see.

SPRING MOUNTAIN RANCH STATE PARK
(875-4141)

Once owned by Howard Hughes and Chet Lauck, Spring Mountain Ranch is a working ranch house open for tours on weekends and holidays. It's a 520-acre oasis at the base of Wilson Cliffs in Red Rock Canyon. There is an outdoor theater for plays and jazz concerts, and a picnic area.

VALLEY OF FIRE STATE PARK
(397-2088)

So named because of the effect of bright sunlight on the red sandstone, Valley of Fire State Park is located 55 miles northeast of Las Vegas on Interstate 15. This park contains dozens of unique geological formations, as well as remnants of ancient Indian civilizations. The visitor center includes an art gallery.

CHRISTMAS TREE PASS
LAUGHLIN CHAMBER OF COMMERCE
(298-2214)

Indian petroglyphs can be seen on the canyon walls of Grapevine Canyon, located north on Highway 163 off Casino Drive. A short hike is required, but signs mark the way. Christmas Tree Pass is another experience to put on your "Don't Miss" list.

CLARK COUNTY HERITAGE MUSEUM
(455-7955)

This museum offers three primary exhibit areas. The first represents units of time in southern Nevada, from dinosaur fossils and Indian cultures to the first white settlers.

Second is Heritage Street, a group of historic commercial and residential buildings. The third is a recreated ghost town featuring several original buildings and railroad cars.

LIED DISCOVERY
CHILDREN'S MUSEUM
(382-3445)

This is a museum where children can understand and appreciate the arts and the basic principles of science. It features 22,000 square feet of exhibit space for hands-on activities and displays in arts, sciences, and humanities. Children are actually invited to touch the exhibits and play with them.

ETHEL M. CHOCOLATE FACTORY
AND CACTUS GARDEN
(458-8864)

The free, self-guided tours of the factory offer a behind-the-scenes look at candy making (Very good candy, I might add). Adjacent to the factory is a lovely display of cactus and botanical gardens featuring over 350 desert plants.

HOOVER DAM
(293-8367)

Hoover Dam is located 27 miles southeast of Las Vegas on the Nevada/Arizona border. Completed in 1935, the 726 foot high dam is considered to be one of the engineering wonders of the world. Not only does the dam help control the Colorado River, it also provides an inexpensive source of electricity which has aided the development of Las Vegas.

MARJORIE BARRICK MUSEUM
OF NATURAL HISTORY
(739-3381)

This museum, located on the campus of the University of Nevada, Las Vegas, offers permanent exhibits on the archeology, geology, and biology of the desert southwest. An outdoor botanical garden and displays of indigenous live animals are also special features. Admission is free.

NEVADA STATE MUSEUM AND
HISTORICAL SOCIETY
(486-5205)

This museum is located in a picturesque lagoon setting in Lorenzi Park.

Three main galleries focus on the history, anthropology, and biology of the area. Two more galleries house changing exhibits on a variety of topics, in addition to a research library and museum store. Many art exhibits of local artists are held at Lorenzi Park.

OLD MORMON FORT
(382-7198)

The Fort, built by the Mormons in 1855, is the oldest historic site in Southern Nevada. The Fort provided shelter for gold seekers and other travelers along the Salt Lake to Los Angeles Trail. It was left to the Indians after the gold rush and later restored and used as a railroad junction post for a railroad that predated the Union Pacific. Turn-of-the-century antiques are displayed and guided tours are available.

OLD NEVADA/BONNIE SPRINGS RANCH
(875-4191)

Located in the natural wonder of Red Rock Canyon, Old Nevada is an adventure into the old west, complete with live shoot-outs, hangings and wooden sidewalks. This full-scale restoration of an old-time Western town features a saloon for adults, an ice cream parlor for children, a wax museum, and 40 historic exhibits and shops. Right next to Old Nevada is Bonnie Springs Ranch, featuring horseback riding, a petting zoo, and dining.

WET 'N WILD
(737-7873)

This 26-acre water park is located on the Strip next to the Sahara Hotel. It has something for everyone from the terrifying Der Stuka, a 76-foot free fall down a watery chute, to a float trip along a 1/3 mile river. Slides, water cannons, rapids, sunbathing, and picnic areas abound at the park.

♥ ♣ ♦ ♠ ♥ ♣ ♦ ♠

SPORTING AREAS

WATER SKIING

Lake Havasu State Park - 1-602-855-7851
Lake Mead National Recreation Area -
    293-8920
Lake Mojave - 1-602-754-3272

SNOW SKIING

Lee Canyon Ski Area/Mt. Charleston
Recreation Area
    Information - 872-5462
    Recorded Ski Information - 658-1927

♥ ♣ ♦ ♠ ♥ ♣ ♦ ♠

GOLF COURSES

ANGEL PARK GOLF CLUB
    100 S. Rampart Blvd.
    Las Vegas, NV 89128
    (702) 254-4653

BLACK MOUNTAIN COUNTRY CLUB
    501 Country Club Drive
    Henderson, NV 89015
    (702) 565-7933

BOULDER CITY GOLF CLUB
    1 Clubhouse Drive
    Boulder City, NV 89005
    (702) 293-9236

CAL-VADA COUNTRY CLUB
　　Red Butte Rd/PO Box 220
　　Pahrump, NV 89041
　　(702) 727-4653

CANYON GATE COUNTRY CLUB
　　2121 Lookout Point
　　Las Vegas, NV 89117
　　(702) 363-4860

CRAIG RANCH GOLF COURSE
　　628 W. Craig Road
　　North Las Vegas, NV 89030
　　(702) 642-9700

DESERT INN COUNTRY CLUB
　　3145 Las Vegas Blvd. S.
　　Las Vegas, NV 89109
　　(702) 733-4444

DESERT ROSE GOLF COURSE
　　5483 Club House Drive
　　Las Vegas, NV 89122
　　(702) 431-4653

JUNIOR GOLF OF SOUTHERN NEVADA
2941 Picasso Circle
Las Vegas, NV 89121
(702) 737-3500

LAS VEGAS COUNTRY CLUB
3000 Joe W. Brown Drive
Las Vegas, NV 89109
(702) 734-1122

LAS VEGAS GOLF CLUB
4349 Vegas Drive
Las Vegas, NV 89108
(702) 646-3003

LEGACY GOLF CLUB
130 Par Excellence Drive
Henderson, NV 89016
(702) 897-2187

LOS PRADOS COUNTRY CLUB
5150 Los Prados Circle
Las Vegas, NV 89130
(702) 645-5696

MIRAGE GOLF CLUB
3650 Las Vegas Blvd. South
Las Vegas, NV 89109
(702) 369-7111

NORTH LAS VEGAS MUNICIPAL GOLF COURSE
324 W. Brooks Avenue
North Las Vegas, NV 89030
(702) 649-7171

PAINTED DESERT GOLF COURSE
5555 Painted Mirage Way
Las Vegas, NV 89129
(702) 645-2568

ROYAL KENFIELD COUNTRY CLUB
1 Royal Kenfield Drive
Henderson, NV 89015
(702) 451-2106

SAHARA COUNTRY CLUB
1911 E. Desert Inn Road
Las Vegas, NV 89109
(702) 796-0016

SPANISH TRAIL COUNTRY CLUB
5050 Spanish Trail Lane
Las Vegas, NV 89113
(702) 364-5050

SUN CITY SUMMERLIN GOLF COURSE
    9201 Del Webb Blvd.
    Las Vegas, NV 89128
    (702) 363-4373

SUNRISE COUNTRY CLUB
    5500 E. Flamingo Road
    Las Vegas, NV 89122
    (702) 456-3160

****

    Some people just play the game. However, the winners are usually those who "know the score".

♥ ♣ ♦ ♠ ♥ ♣ ♦ ♠

HELP KEEP AMERICA BEAUTIFUL

Two years ago, a retired couple from the Midwest arrived in Las Vegas to spend a pleasant winter. They acquired an apartment just two blocks off the Las Vegas Strip. Due to the mild climate of our winter evenings, they began taking long evening walks. Their strolls took them past the Maxim Hotel, Bourbon Street Hotel, and the Barbary Coast. They would turn right, onto the Strip, and proceed past the Flamingo Hilton, the Imperial Palace, the Holiday Inn, and the Sands Hotel. Some evenings they would walk on the opposite side of the street which would take them past Bally's, Caesars Palace, and the Mirage.

Along all of these trails they noticed hotel bar glasses scattered on the lawns and beside the sidewalks. Having come from a clean community in the Midwest, this littering disturbed them. After awhile, as they walked, they began collecting the glasses. At the end of three months, they found they had acquired over 400. A friend suggested they could open their own bar. Instead, they took all the glasses home with them to the Midwest. The glasses with hotel/casino logos were given to family and friends as souvenirs. The rest were given to a local charity. It seemed like a nice and appropriate way to deal with the problem of keeping Las Vegas clean.

****

Watch for big problems because they often disguise big opportunities.

♥ ♣ ♦ ♠ ♥ ♣ ♦ ♠

SOCIAL AND CHARITABLE ORGANIZATIONS

The churches of our community offer many social activities for their members. There is also a large number of clubs and charitable organizations which would welcome you with open arms. If you are the type to volunteer, the United Way has a list of all the charitable organizations who need assistance. On the volunteer list, there is something for everyone. No matter what it is that you are good at, or like to do, the United Way can point you in the direction where your talents can be utilized.

There are many clubs and organizations in Las Vegas with which you can become associated. It is a great way to meet people and make friends. It is also a good start at establishing your new life in Las Vegas. Here is just a partial listing of some of the clubs in our fine community:

Christian Women's Club
Clark County Cloggers
Cribbage Club
Elks
Friday Night Dance Club
German-American Social Club

Italian-American Club
Italian-American Professional &
    Executive Association
    (Augustus Society)
Las Vegas Friendship Club
Las Vegas Jaycees
Las Vegas Ski Club
Lions Club
Luncheon Optimists Club
Matinee Swing Club
New Mexico Club of Nevada
New York Club
Parents Without Partners
Rotary Club
Scrabble Club
Sons of Erin
Sons of Italy
Sports Car Club of America
Square Dance Club
Toastmasters International
VFW

There are numerous other clubs and organizations in Las Vegas. The list could go on and on. A listing of up-coming activities for many organizations is published in the local newspapers.

Our libraries and the University offer a large number of entertainment programs every month. These include symphonies, the ballet, theater productions, art exhibits, lectures, special films, and so much more. With all the activities going on in Las Vegas daily, you could attend some function every day, and be thoroughly entertained.

♥ ♣ ♦ ♠ ♥ ♣ ♦ ♠

AUTOMOBILE RENTING & LEASING

If you need to lease an auto while visiting Las Vegas, we have all the major auto rental agencies, along with a lot of smaller ones. It is usually smart to call ahead to rent one before you arrive, because with all the large conventions booked in Las Vegas, the many agencies sometimes run short of available rentals.

♥ ♣ ♦ ♠ ♥ ♣ ♦ ♠

DRIVING WITH CAUTION

It's a little different driving in the rain in Las Vegas, as compared to driving in the rain in the Midwest or the East. Since Las Vegas gets very little rain, our streets tend to become very slick when it does start sprinkling. The reason for this is that oil becomes imbedded in the paved streets over a long, dry period, and when moisture finally hits, it mixes with the oil to produce a very slick, almost icy-like situation. Ambulances are kept very busy on a rainy day as far too many accidents occur. The same thing happens when...Actually, I should say "if"...we get snow in the city.

As a survivor of a drastic automobile accident, which happened on a rainy evening, I feel inclined to warn everyone of the dangers of our wet streets. You must drive with caution. You may think that you are a very good driver, but all too often, it is the "other guy" you have to worry about. In my case, the accident wasn't my fault. It doesn't make any difference whose fault it was. The fact remains that it took nine months of being laid up with terrible pain...nine whole, wasted months out of my life. Perhaps if I had been driving a little slower, I could have avoided the driver who spun out from a side street.

♥ ♣ ♦ ♠ ♥ ♣ ♦ ♠

MISCELLANEOUS INFORMATION

To acquire a local phone number in Las Vegas, dial 555-1212. There is a 25¢ charge for this service.

To get the time and temperature, dial 118.

For emergencies, dial 9-1-1. The Metropolitan Police Department number for non-emergencies is 795-3111.

Las Vegas has two major daily newspapers - the *Las Vegas Sun*, and the *Review/Journal*. There are also several neighborhood newspapers, as well as newspapers geared exclusively for seniors and tourists. To subscribe to the *Las Vegas Sun*, dial (702) 383-0400, and for the *Review/Journal*, call (702) 383-0211. These two major newspapers combine on Saturday and Sunday to issue just one newspaper on those days. A good way to acquaint yourself with Las Vegas is to subscribe to the Sunday paper. In addition, the Sunday paper is normally packed with "Help Wanted" ads. This can assist the potential job-seeker in learning what type of jobs are available in the area. The monthly subscription rate for the Sunday paper to be mailed to you out-of-state is around $12.00.

A LAS VEGAS SUCCESS STORY

At age 9, he had a paper route. At age 12, he became a delivery man for a fruit stand. By age 16, he was managing a produce market, and at age 20, he became the assistant manager of a large supermarket. These jobs left no time for Tony Tegano to acquire a high school education, but his early training in the good old "American Work Ethic" has lead him to be the owner of the largest pool building company in Las Vegas.

Tony arrived in Las Vegas from Brooklyn, New York in 1959. As most people did in those days, he entered the gaming industry as a dealer. He lived on the $1.00 per hour wages for awhile, but even in gaming he was quickly promoted. During his years in gaming, he acquired a promotion to "pit boss". He also acquired a very beautiful showgirl as his wife. Not only was she gorgeous, Robin was also extremely intelligent. She proved to be a great asset to Tony as they forged ahead and opened their own pool building business. Today, Tango Pools does more than 60% of the commercial pool building in Las Vegas, and has a corner on the residential market too.

Tony also has invested in a custom cabinet shop which designs and builds a lot of the custom cabinetry for many of the major hotels in Las Vegas. Before money can grow on trees, the seeds have to be planted, and the seeds were long hours (often seven days a week) and backbreaking hard work for both Tony and Robin. "Hard work is what it's all about," Tony says. It's also about integrity.

A few summers ago, numerous homeowners were stung by two different pool building companies that went out of business unexpectedly. The homeowners had given the pool companies hefty deposits and were left with nothing but big holes in their backyards. Tony came to the rescue and completed many of the pools for just the balances that would have been paid to the other companies. This resulted in losses for Tango Pools because the original deposits by the homeowners to the other pool companies had, in most cases, been large. Very little work had been completed on their pools. Tony did the work for two reasons: (1) He said he knew how he would feel if something like that happened to him; and (2) He didn't want the pool building industry in Las Vegas to get a bad name.

Tony and Robin's generosity far exceeds the normal. They are both actively involved in many charitable organizations in the city and believe in giving back to a community that has been good to them. This city is made up of many successful, caring residents just like Tony and Robin Tegano.

****

Many street corners in Las Vegas, like other major cities, are dotted with homeless and unemployed, holding signs which read, "Will work for food", etc. Some time ago, one such sign caught the attention of every passerby. The sign read, "Unemployed! Will work for $40,000 a year." The sign was held by a young man dressed in a nice suit and tie. Rumor has it, he acquired a job in marketing shortly thereafter. Innovative idea, wouldn't you say?

♥ ♣ ♦ ♠ ♥ ♣ ♦ ♠

HOW IT ALL STARTED

In 1970, my husband and I moved to Las Vegas to open an Italian Sandwich Shop. To save money on kitchen equipment, we purchased used stoves, freezers, refrigerators, and other equipment in our home town of Chicago. We had it shipped to Las Vegas. Upon arrival, we were informed that Las Vegas had special regulations. Every piece of equipment used in the shop needed to be "NSF Approved". Our equipment was not, since it was from Chicago. We were told we could use none of it, and would have to buy all new equipment if we wanted to open the shop. So $60,000 later, we opened the Sandwich Shop. The used equipment that we had bought in Chicago for $12,000 was finally sold for ten cents on the dollar. We were also unexpectedly informed that we needed two stainless steel exhaust ducts. These were to run from the ceiling of our Shop through the top of the roof. We were in a two-story building, on the first floor, so these ducts each had to be thirteen feet high. Would you care to guess what 26 feet of solid stainless steel duct work cost?

Those were only two examples of the nightmares we incurred in setting up a business in Las Vegas. There were a lot more, I assure you. But we were new to Las Vegas and didn't have anyone to advise us. Just getting the Sandwich Shop open cost $60,000 more than we had budgeted. Our first year was very rough. You have to sell a lot of sandwiches (at that time we charged 89¢ for a huge sandwich with fries) to make up for the initial business investment. Business was good, but it wasn't <u>that</u> good!

I worked seven days a week in the Sandwich Shop. My husband decided he had better get another job to support us and recoup some of our investment. Many of our customers were hotel-casino executives from the Strip. My husband decided to ask one of them for a job dealing blackjack. He liked to play cards and was very good with card tricks. The casino executive said, "No. That's not how it works. First you must go to dealing school. Then you try to get a dealing job downtown and 'break in' for a year. After that you can apply for a job on the Strip." Dealing school meant another out-of-pocket expense, but my husband decided he should do it.

So off to school he went. Six weeks later, when he graduated, he was fortunate to find a job at the El Cortez Hotel where he earned $1.65 an hour plus approximately $3.00 a day in tips (on a "good" day). For years, we had heard stories about casino dealers in Las Vegas making BIG money and fabulous tips, so talk about "getting the air let out of your balloon"! This was very depressing.

It was almost as bad as the time my husband was changing the hot grease in the french fryer at the Sandwich Shop. The grease splashed over his arm and totally fried it. I grabbed a pound of butter and rubbed it over the burn. Then I rushed him to the hospital. The emergency room doctor let me know, in no uncertain terms, how stupid I was. They packed his arm in ice trying to get rid of the sizzling butter. That was embarrassing for me. All I had tried to do was help.

I missed Chicago and our friends. I felt if we were in Chicago, we could have gone to our nice family doctor. At least he would have been kind to me, even if he did think I was stupid. Another thought occurred to me too. We wouldn't have ended up $60,000 over budget opening a sandwich shop there, because someone would have given us advice and assistance before we made a mistake. And if we were still in Chicago, my husband wouldn't have had to go to a special school to get a job. We had enough friends that he could have had any kind of work, AND they would have trained him on the job.

We had three years of financial struggles and many heartbreaking moments before the tide began to turn. During those three years, we worked like fools and learned a lot. Many people would have packed up and gone back home, but we were too proud. Besides, we got a kick out of those winter phone calls from Chicago friends. They were shoveling snow, while we were enjoying 70° temperatures, and basking by the pool.

Due to the hardships we had endured during those first three years, we were sympathetic to any Las Vegas newcomers who were confused and frustrated. We didn't want to see anyone have the kinds of problems we did. Whenever we could, we went out of our way to help newcomers avoid the horrors and pitfalls of relocating to a new city.

If, after reading this directory, you find that there is still more information that you need, you may call our local Chamber of Commerce at (702) 735-1616. They will try to help you in any way they can. Or you can write to us at:

Information and Assistance Network
3675 S. Rainbow
Suite 107, Box 122
Las Vegas, NV 89103

GOOD LUCK!

♥ ♣ ♦ ♠ ♥ ♣ ♦ ♠

NOTES

NOTES

NOTES

NOTES